# DUTCH SOCCER DRILLS

## Henny Kormelink

**Library of Congress
Cataloging - in - Publication Data**

Dutch Soccer Drills
Vol. 5
by Henny Kormelink

ISBN 1-59164-102-0
Library of Congress Control Number: 96-41894
© 2006

*Editing*
Bryan R. Beaver

*Translation from Dutch*
Dave Brandt

*Printed by*
Data Reproductions
Auburn, Michigan

Reedswain Publishing
562 Ridge Road
Spring City, PA 19475
www. reedswain.com
info@reedswain.com

# CONTENTS

**OBJECTIVE:**    Improving faking skills.

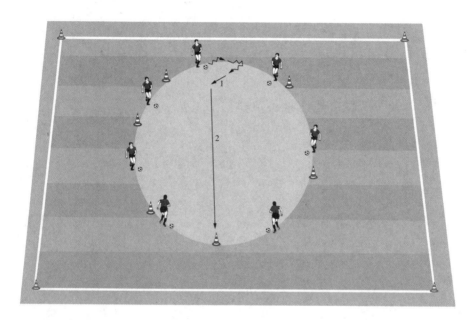

**ORGANIZATION:**    Mark out a big circle with tall cones.

**INSTRUCTIONS:**

- Each players has a ball and dribbles round the edge of the circle.
- At a sign from the coach, each player drags the ball behind his standing leg, controls the ball with one touch and passes to a cone on the opposite side of the circle.
- If the ball hits the cone, the player scores on point (the pass can be along the ground or through the air).
- When the balls have passed the cones, each player takes another ball.

# DRIBBLING

**OBJECTIVE:**     Learning to score after a fake movement.

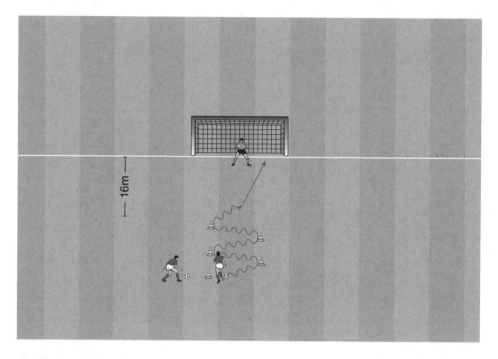

16m

**ORGANIZATION:**
- A goalkeeper stands in the goal. A path is marked about 15 yards from the goal by six cones at intervals of 3 yards.
- The players stand 5 yards behind the marked path. Each player has a ball.
- A player dribbles along the path, faking to one side at each cone.
- After the last fake, the player shoots at the goal.

Variation
Carry out different dribbling movements and fakes at the cones (step-over, scissor, etc.).

# DRIBBLING

**OBJECTIVE:** Learning to score after a fake movement.

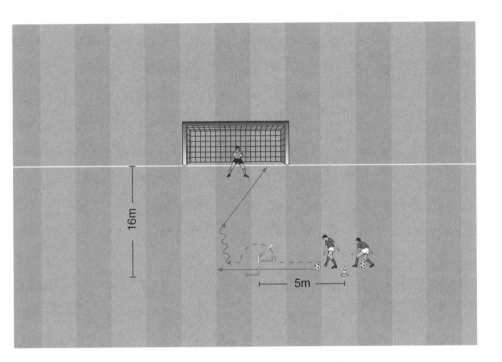

16m

5m

**ORGANIZATION:**
- A goalkeeper stands in the goal. A low hurdle is positioned 15 yards in front of the goal.
- The players stand 5 yards away from the hurdle. Each player has a ball.
- The first player runs with the ball toward the hurdle, passes the ball under the hurdle and jumps over the hurdle.
- The player then cuts the ball with the inside or outside of the foot and shoots at the goal.

**INSTRUCTIONS:**
- Take care not to land on the ball after jumping (injury risk).
- Run into space with the ball and accelerate.

# DRIBBLING

Improving ability to take the ball past an opponent in one-against-one situations.

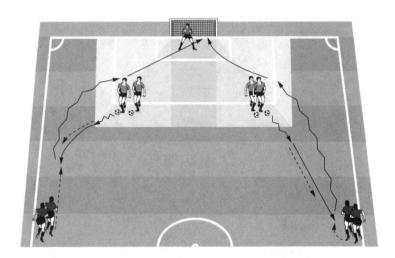

**ORGANIZATION:**
- Use the 3 attacking zones
- Two defenders stand at the left corner of the penalty area and two at the right.
- Two attackers stand at the left edge of the center line and two at the right.
- The defenders must obtain a ball somehow to start the drill (by fetching one out of the goal, or receiving a pass from the other side of the pitch).

**INSTRUCTIONS:**
- The attacker moves into space to receive a pass.
- He receives the ball and takes it on the run.
- The defender moves to cut off the attacker and tries to stop the attacker from taking the ball past him.
- The attacker tries to go past the defender by accelerating a faking.
- The attacker can go through the middle or down the flank.
- If the defender wins the ball, he passes to the other side of the pitch.

# PASSING

**OBJECTIVE:**
- Improving passing technique.
- Improving "receive and go" technique.

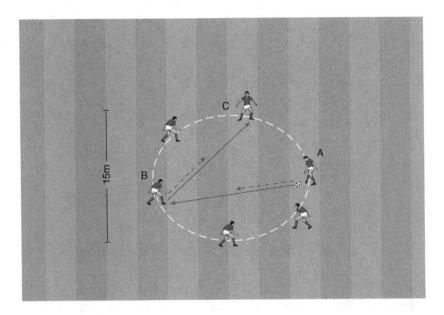

**ORGANIZATION:**
- Six players (A-F) form a circle 15 yards wide. Player A has the ball.
- Player A passes to player B and runs after the pass.
- Player A can perform various running movements as he follows the ball.

Variation
- Player A passes to player B, who passes back to A.
- Player B passes to player C, who starts a new combination by playing a long pass.

**INSTRUCTIONS:**
- Look beyond the ball so that you can see the other player.
- Accelerate after passing the ball.

# PASSING 6

**OBJECTIVE:** Improving passing skills.

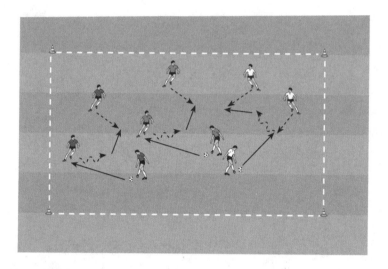

**ORGANIZATION:** Groups of three players in one quarter of a full sized field. Each player has a ball.

**INSTRUCTIONS:**
- Practice freely with the ball, then carry out individual exercises.
- At a sign from the coach, the players combine at high speed for about 10 seconds, then play the ball to each other at a more relaxed speed.
- One player must pass with his first touch, while the other are allowed 2 touches, then the players change roles within the group.
- Pass the ball through the air with all players in motion.
- Running into space and calling for a pass. One of the 3 players calls for a pass through the air by accelerating into space. He receives and runs with the ball, then passes it through the air again.

**OBJECTIVE:**    Improving passing and kicking technique.

**ORGANIZATION:**
- Continuous drill.
- Minimum of 10 players.
- Playing area 30 x 40 yards.
- Each player runs after the pass.

**INSTRUCTIONS:**
- Player 1 plays the ball in to player 2.
- Player 2 plays the ball back to 1.
- Player 1 passes to player 3.
- Player 3 turns so that he is at an angle to the path of the ball, receives the pass and runs towards the cone, where the sequence starts again.
- Start off slowly and build up speed.
- Free play, then reduce the number of ball contacts (2-touch play, for example).
- Start with large intervals between the players, then reduce the distance between them.
- Start with one station, then add another.

# PASSING 8

**OBJECTIVE:** Improving passing and kicking technique with the emphasis on the receiver of the pass. In particular, improving the timing of the initial run and the preparation of the player who is to receive the pass.

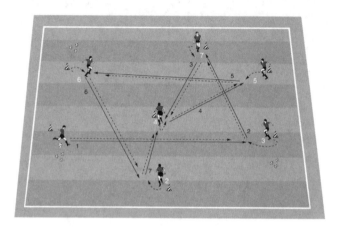

**ORGANIZATION:**
- Playing area 35 yards by 30 yards.
- 5 to 7 players.
- 1 ball for the drill, several balls nearby.
- 7 cones at variable intervals. The central cone can be removed once the drill is in progress
- Duration of the drill: 20 to 25 minutes.
- The sequence of passes can be left to the players. In the diagram it is 1-3-7-4-5-6-2-7, who has taken over the position of player 4.
- Rotation sequence: same as passing sequence.

**INSTRUCTIONS:**
Passer:
- Must be fully concentrated on what he is doing.
- Using the inside of the foot, pass firmly along the ground to the receiver's feet.

Receiver:
- Don't just call for the ball but run into space and indicate how and when the ball must be played. Signal your intentions!
- Control the ball with your first touch.

# PASSING

**OBJECTIVE:** Improving passing and kicking technique

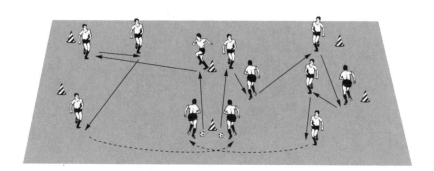

**ORGANIZATION:**
- Passing and kicking in a Y-shaped pattern.
- Keep moving through to the next cone.
- When you come from one side, join onto the other side.
- The intervals between cones should be match-relevant (15-20 yards).
- 'Fixed' drills first. Later the players can be allowed to decide what they want to do through communication and observation.

**INSTRUCTIONS:**
- Good technique.
- Communication.
- Concentration.
- Follow on after checking away.
- Stay focused, never more than 5 or 6 passes.
- Keep communicating.
- A shot at goal or a pass into the goal can be in corporated into the drill.

**OBJECTIVE:**

Involvement of third man.

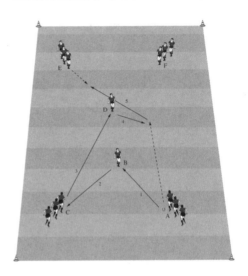

**ORGANIZATION:**

- Length of field 40 yards, width 20 yards.
- 14 players.
- 2 players at each outside cone.
- 2 fixed players in the center.

**INSTRUCTIONS:**

- Player A passes to the central player B.
- Player B lays the ball off to the third man C.
- Player C plays the ball to the central player D.
- Player D lays the ball off to the incoming player A.
- Player A plays the ball diagonally to E with his first touch.
- We then start on the other side.
- The two central players turn to face the other direction.
- Player E plays the ball to the central player D.
- Player D lays the ball off to player F.
- Player F plays the ball to central player B.
- Player B lays the ball off to the incoming player E.
- Player E plays the ball diagonally to player A.

Rotate one position:
Central players remain in position. C–A–F–E–C.

# PASSING

**OBJECTIVE:**
- Accurate passing.
- Good first touch.

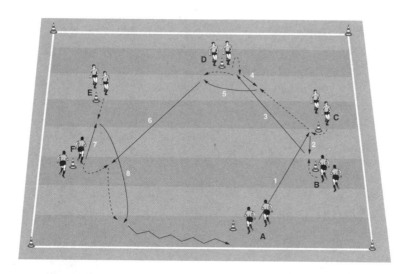

**ORGANIZATION:**
- Everyone moves to next position after playing the ball.
- Player C determines when the next sequence of passes starts.

**INSTRUCTIONS:**
- Player A passes to player C, who first checks away and then checks back to receive the pass.
- Player C lays the ball off to player B.
- Player B passes to player D, who first checks away and then checks back to receive the pass.
- Player D lays the ball off to the incoming player C and runs into space.
- Player C completes a 1-2 combination by playing the ball into the path of player D.
- Player D passes to player F, who first checks away and then checks back to receive the pass.
- Player F lays the ball off to player E.
- Player E plays a forward pass for player F to run onto.
- Player F cuts the ball back and runs back with the ball to player A.

# PASSING

**OBJECTIVE:**   Improving passing and kicking technique.

**ORGANIZATION:**
- Continuous drill.
- Minimum of 10 players.
- Playing area 30 x 40 yards.
- Each player runs after the pass.

**INSTRUCTIONS:**
- Player 1 plays the ball in to player 2.
- Player 2 makes a half turn and plays the ball to player 3.
- Player 3 makes a half turn, controls the ball and runs with the ball to the other side of the pitch, where the drill starts again.
- Start off slowly and build up speed.
- Free play, then reduce the number of ball contacts (two-touch play, for example).
- Start with wide gaps between the players and decrease the gaps gradually.
- Start with one station, then introduce a second.

**OBJECTIVE:**   Improving passing and kicking technique.

**ORGANIZATION:**
- Continuous drill.
- Minimum of 10 players.
- Playing area 30 x 40 yards.
- Each player follows the ball.

**INSTRUCTIONS:**
- Player 1 plays the ball in to player 2.
- Player 2 makes a half turn and plays the ball to player 3.
- Player 3 lays the ball off to player 2, who plays it into the path of player 3. Player 3 runs with the ball to the other side of the field.
- Start off slowly and build up speed.
- Free play, then reduce the number of ball contacts (two-touch play, for example).
- Start with wide gaps between the players and decrease the gaps gradually.
- Start with one station, then introduce a second.

# PASSING

**OBJECTIVE:** Improving passing and kicking technique.

**ORGANIZATION:**
- Continuous drill.
- Minimum of 10 players.
- Playing area 30 x 40 yards.
- Each player follows the ball.

**INSTRUCTIONS:**
- Player 1 plays the ball in to player 2.
- Player 2 lays the ball off to player 1.
- Player 1 plays the ball forward to player 3 and runs forward to support him.
- The ball is passed to player 2 again, who again runs with the ball toward the other side of the field.
- Start off slowly and build up speed.
- Free play, then reduce the number of ball contacts (two-touch play, for example).
- Start with wide gaps between the players and decrease the gaps gradually.
- Start with one station, then introduce a second.

# PASSING

**OBJECTIVE:**  Improving passing and kicking technique.

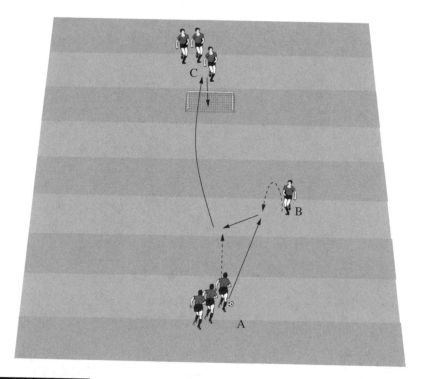

**ORGANIZATION:**
- Practice field.
- Three groups of players.
- Player C stands about 5 yards from the goal.

**INSTRUCTIONS:**
- Player A plays the ball to the inside foot of player B, who first checks away and then checks back to receive the pass.
- Player B lays the ball off diagonally to the foot with which the incoming player A passed.
- Player A passes the ball through the air to player C, who is standing behind the small junior goal.
- Player C tries to score.

# PASSING

**OBJECTIVE:** Improving passing and kicking technique.

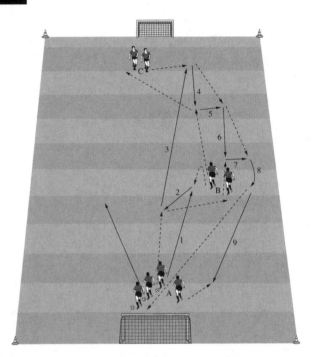

**ORGANIZATION:**
- Player B checks away and then checks back to receive a pass from player A (start position).
- Player A passes firmly to player B.
- Player B lays the ball off to the incoming player A, makes a half turn and runs toward player C.
- Player A passes firmly to player C, who is calling for the ball, and runs to the back of the B group.
- Player C plays a 1-2 combination with player B, then player B runs to the back of the C group.
- C plays a 1-2 combination with the second player B.
- Player C passes to the player calling for the ball near the start position.
- Player C runs to the back of group A beside the start position.
- As soon as there is enough space, the second player in Group A starts down the other side of the field.

**OBJECTIVE:** Improving passing and kicking technique.

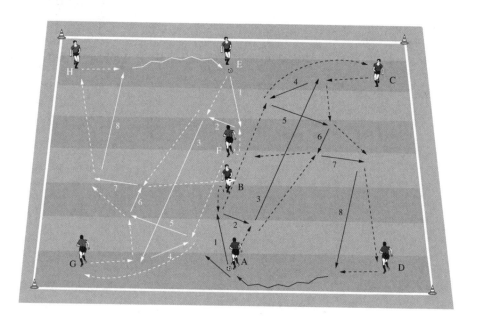

**ORGANIZATION:**

- Players A and E start the continuous course simultaneously.
- Player A plays the ball to B, who first checks away and then checks back to receive the pass.
- Player B lays the ball off to the incoming player A, who then passes to player C.
- Player B runs into space and calls for a pass from player C, who plays the ball back to him.
- Player B plays the ball diagonally to player C, who has run into space.
- Player C plays a 1-2 combination with player A, who has made a forward run.
- Player C plays the ball to player D, who is making a forward run.

Moving to the next position:
- Player A moves to the position of player B.
- Player B moves to the position of player C.
- Player C moves to the position of player D.
- Player D runs with the ball to the position of player A, but now starts the course on the left side.
- Player E therefore starts the course simultaneously on the left on the other side.

Very complex, and with sufficient players the drill can even be played with 4 balls.

# PASSING 18

**OBJECTIVE:** Improving technical skills such as passing and receiving.

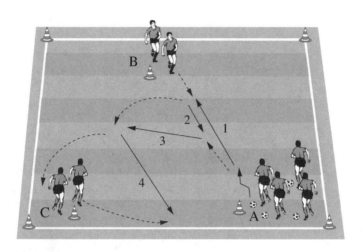

**ORGANIZATION:**
- Triangle.
- 4-8 players per triangle.

**INSTRUCTIONS:**
Technique
Two-footed
- 'Use both feet. Keep the ball circulating quickly. Try to use the inside of your foot as much as possible.'
Lay-off
- 'Lay the ball off with feeling. Take the pace off the ball. This helps your teammate.'
Tactics
Timing
- 'Don't make your run too early, because the pass might then arrive behind you.' Correct foot.
- 'Play the ball to your teammate's inside foot, but try to stay on the edge of the triangle.'

Improving passing and kicking technique.

**ORGANIZATION:**

- Player 1 plays a 1-2 combination with player 2 and passes to player 3, who first checks away and then checks back to receive the pass.
- Player 3 lays the ball off to the incoming player 2, who passes to player 4.
- Player 4 plays the ball to player 5, who first checks away and then checks back to receive the pass.
- Player 4 makes a forward run, receives the pass and passes into the path of player 5, who runs for goal and tries to score.

Variation
- Player 3 plays the ball back to player 2.
- Player 2 passes to winger 5 or 6.
- The winger passes to the incoming player 4 or 7, who tries to score.

**OBJECTIVE:**

To improve passing and kicking technique in groups of 2, with the help of 2 "lay-off" players, after a long ball from the goalkeeper.

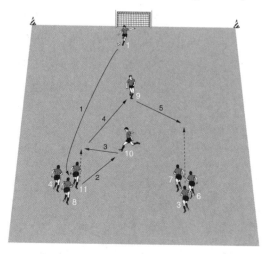

**ORGANIZATION:**

- The goalkeeper sends a long ball to player 11.
- 11 plays a 1-2 combination with lay-off player 10.
- Player 11 passes to lay-off player 9.
- 9 plays the ball square for the advancing player 7.

**INSTRUCTIONS:**

- Good ball control after long ball from goalkeeper.
- Lay-off players 10 and 9 check away and then check back to create space.
- Cooperation between players 9 and 10, who maintain their distance from each other.
- Play in the first and second man after receiving
- Keep the ball circulating quickly.
- Players 9 and 10 should pass to the correct foot of the receiving player.
- Play in the first and second man after receiving
- Move up quickly to support the move.

Special aspects
- The goalkeeper can kick the ball from the ground or from his hands or he can throw it.
- The 2 players switch positions.

**OBJECTIVE:**

To improve passing and kicking technique in groups of 2, with the help of 2 "lay-off" players, after a long ball from the goalkeeper.

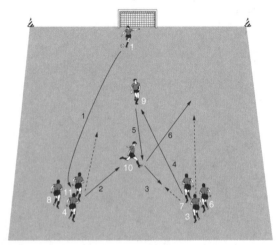

**ORGANIZATION:**

- The goalkeeper sends a long ball to player 11.
- 11 passes to lay-off player 10, who lays the ball off to the incoming player 7.
- Player 7 passes to lay-off player 9.
- 9 lays the ball back to lay-off player 10.
- 10 passes to the incoming player 7.

**INSTRUCTIONS:**

- Good ball control after long ball from goalkeeper.
- Lay-off players 10 and 9 check away and check back to create space.
- Cooperation between players 9 and 10, who maintain their distance from each other.
- Play in the first and second man after receiving
- Keep the ball circulating quickly.
- Players 9 and 10 should lay the ball off to the correct foot of the receiving player.
- Play in the first and second man after receiving
- Move up quickly to support the move.

Special aspects
- The goalkeeper can kick the ball out from the ground or from his hands or he can throw it.
- The 2 players switch positions.

# PASSING    22

**OBJECTIVE:**
To improve passing and kicking technique in groups of 2, with the help of 2 "lay-off" players, after a long ball from the goalkeeper.

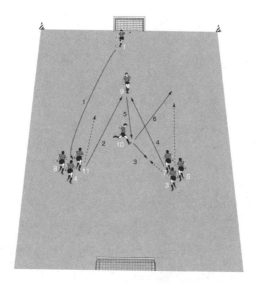

**ORGANIZATION:**
- The goalkeeper sends a long ball to player 11.
- Direct pass to player 9 (miss out 10), who lays the ball off to player 10, who plays the ball square to the advancing player 7.

**INSTRUCTIONS:**
- Good ball control after long ball from goalkeeper.
- Lay-off players 10 and 9 check away and check back to create space.
- Cooperation between players 9 and 10, who maintain their distance from each other.
- Play in the first and second man after receiving
- Keep the ball circulating quickly.
- Players 9 and 10 should lay the ball off to the correct foot of the receiving player.
- Move up quickly to support the move.

Special aspects
- The goalkeeper can kick the ball out from the ground or from his hands or he can throw it.
- The 2 players switch positions.

**OBJECTIVE:**
- Improving first touch with either foot when receiving a pass
- Improving passing with either foot.

**ORGANIZATION:**
- Use an area as long as half of a full sized pitch.
- Work on the left and the right, depending on the number of players.
- Post several players at each position to speed things up.

**INSTRUCTIONS:**
- Player A starts with the ball.
- Player B checks away and checks back to receive the ball.
- Player B stands at an angle to the path of the ball, takes the ball with the inside of the foot and turns towards the flank in one movement (first touch), then passes the ball to player C with the other foot (second touch).
- Player C checks away and checks back to receive the ball.
- Player C sprints with the ball to the position of player A.
- Each player moves to the next position.

# PASSING 24

**OBJECTIVE:**
- Improving first touch with either foot when receiving a pass
- Improving passing with either foot.

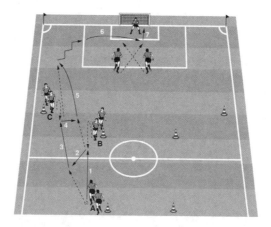

**ORGANIZATION:**
- Area is about half of a full sized pitch.
- Work on the left and the right, depending on the number of players.
- Post several players at each position.

**INSTRUCTIONS:**
- Player A plays a 1-2 combination with player B.
- Player A passes to player C, who checks away and then checks back to receive the ball.
- Player C plays a 1-2 combination with player B.
- Reverse the direction of play, or work on both sides of the playing area.
- Increase the distances between the players (more risk in the passing).
- Decrease the distances between the players (more precision required).
- Work with players in fixed positions (no moving to the next position).
- Player C tries to score, or he crosses and the two strikers try to score.
- The strikers cross as they run in at the goal.
- With or without defenders in front of the goal.
- Alternate shooting on the ground and in the air.
- The player on the left flank becomes the outside right when the direction of play is reversed.

**OBJECTIVE:** Improving passing and kicking technique, with shot on goal.

**ORGANIZATION:**
- 4:3:3 formation with an advanced striker and a holding midfielder in front of the defensive line.
- The holding midfielder 6 plays the ball to midfielder 10, who plays it back to him; player 6 then passes to the striker.
- Player 9 lays the ball off for midfielder 8, who is making a forward run.
- Player 8 shoots at goal.

**INSTRUCTIONS:**
- The first pass from player 6 to player 10 must be firm.
- Player 6 must take up position correctly to receive the return pass.
- Player 9 must check away and check back to create space at the right moment.
- Player 8 must call, indicating where he wants the ball, when he makes his forward run.
- If player 9 lays the ball off square, it is easier for an opponent to intercept.
- Player 9 should therefore play the ball back at an angle.

Improving passing and kicking technique, with shot on goal.

**ORGANIZATION:**
- 4:3:3 formation with an advanced striker and an attacking midfielder behind him.
- Player 4 passes to player 10.
- Player 10 lays the ball off to player 6.
- Player 6 passes to the advanced striker 9.
- At the same moment player 8 makes a forward run.
- Player 9 passes to player 10 or 8.

**INSTRUCTIONS:**
- Focus on passing.
- Pass to the correct foot (or pass just in front of the receiver)

# PASSING

**OBJECTIVE:**   Improving passing to the winger, making a run and crossing the ball.

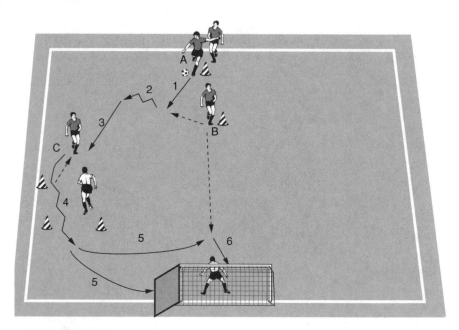

**ORGANIZATION:**
- Player A passes into the path of the striker B.
- Player B makes a half-turn and passes to the advancing winger C.
- Player C makes a run to the end line and scores in the side net or crosses the ball.
- Striker B, who is making a run toward the goal, tries to score from the cross.

**INSTRUCTIONS:**
- Use your right foot to pass to the left, and your left foot to pass to the right.
- First pass should be very firm.

Improving passing to the winger, making a run and crossing the ball.

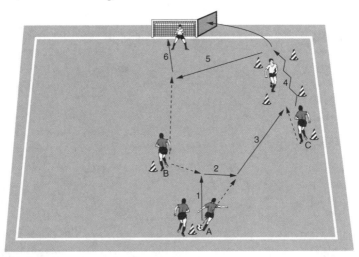

**ORGANIZATION:**
- Player A plays the ball into the path of striker B and makes a forward run.
- Player B lays the ball off into the path of player A.
- Player A passes the ball forward into the path of winger C, who is making a run down the flank.
- Player C makes a run to the end line and scores in the side net or crosses the ball.
- Striker B, who is making a run toward the goal, tries to score from the cross.

**INSTRUCTIONS:**
- Check away and check back to create space.
- Keep the ball circulating.
- Turn towards the flank and look up.
- Lay the ball off into the receiver's path.
- Don't arrive too early in front of the goal.

Variations:
- Different types of passes.
- A player defends the line between 2 cones.
- The defender stands in a zone.
- Introduce a free defender, who can score.
- Score with a header.
- Do the drill down the left and the right flank.

# PASSING

**OBJECTIVE:** Improving passing to the winger, making a run and crossing the ball.

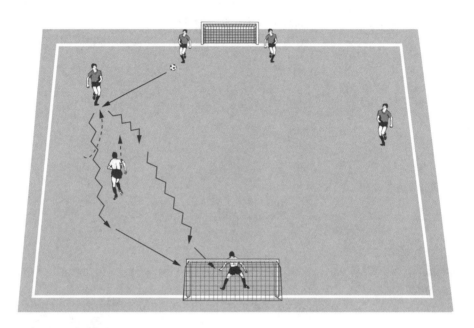

**ORGANIZATION:**
- The ball is played to the feet of the striker.
- The defender can move as soon as the ball is played to the attacker.
- The winger tries to make a run.
- The goalkeeper is only allowed to defend the center goal.
- The defender can score in the empty goal.
- Start alternately on the right and the left flanks.

**INSTRUCTIONS:**
- Check away and check back to create space.
- Take the pass with the outside foot.
- Make a run.
- Threaten to cut inside/outside.
- Dribbling technique.

# PASSING 30

**OBJECTIVE:** Improving passing to the winger, making a run and crossing the ball.

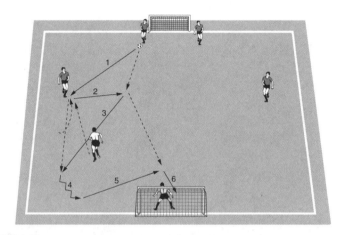

**ORGANIZATION:**
- The start player plays the ball to the feet of the winger and starts a forward run.
- The defender can move as soon as the ball is played to the winger.
- The winger squares the ball into the path of the start player.
- The start player passes back to the winger, who stays on the flank.
- The winger makes a forward run with the ball and crosses to the start player, who tries to score.
- The goalkeeper is only allowed to defend the center goal.
- The defender can score in the empty goal.
- Start alternately on the right and the left flanks.

**INSTRUCTIONS:**
- The position of the defender:
  - if he stays close to the winger, there is space behind his back.
  - if he does not, the ball can be played to the winger's feet.
- The second attacker takes up a position that forces the defender to make a choice.
- The goalkeeper dribbles the ball into play.

**OBJECTIVE:** Improving passing to the winger, making a run and crossing the ball.

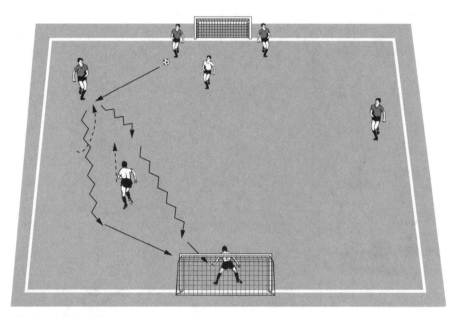

**ORGANIZATION:**
- The ball is played to the feet of the winger.
- One of the two defenders can move as soon as the ball is played to the winger.
- The winger tries to make a run.
- The goalkeeper is only allowed to defend the center goal.
- The defender can score in the empty goal.
- Start alternately on the right and the left flanks.
- This drill produces a lot of one-against-one situations.

**INSTRUCTIONS:**
- Act quickly to get the ball into space.
- The players must make use of the space to help each other to escape the defenders.

**OBJECTIVE:**
Improving passing to the winger, making a run and crossing the ball.

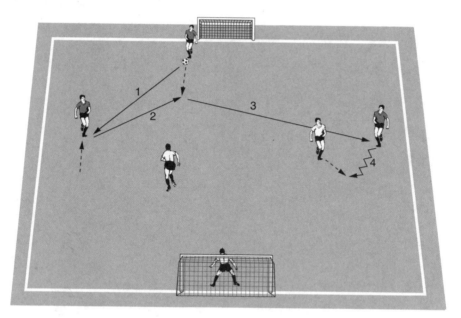

**ORGANIZATION:**
- 2 wingers with 2 defenders and 1 support player.
- Cooperation between the winger and the support player, and switching the play from flank to flank, are the essentials of this drill.

**INSTRUCTIONS:**
- The support player makes sure that the winger can always pass the ball back to him.
- The 2 wingers check away and check back again to create space.
- The ball can be played into the space behind the defender or to the winger's feet.

# PASSING

**OBJECTIVE:** Improving passing to the winger, making a run and crossing the ball.

**ORGANIZATION:**
- The third defender joins in when the first pass is played in by the support player.
- The drill then follows.
- This drill produces a lot of one-against-one situations.

**INSTRUCTIONS:**
- The players must make use of the space to help each other to escape the defenders.
- Checking away and back again is crucial to creating the space needed to escape from defenders.
- The position and free space determine how the passes are made.

# PASSING

**34**

**OBJECTIVE:** Improving passing to the winger, making a run and crossing the ball.

**ORGANIZATION:**
- An advanced striker joins the three players.
- The fourth defender joins in when the first pass is made.

**INSTRUCTIONS:**
- The advanced striker acts as a support player in 1-2 combinations when the winger has the ball, or he creates space to enable the winger to make a run.
- The striker must remain well upfield!

**OBJECTIVE:** Improving passing and kicking technique, with shot a goal.

**ORGANIZATION:**
- Half of a full sized pitch.
- Large goal.
- Sufficient balls and cones.

**INSTRUCTIONS:**
- Player A must start at the correct moment when player G or player H plays the ball into his path.
- Player H must take care to play the ball at the right pace into player A's path.
- Player A crosses the ball to the goalkeeper in the field, who catches the high ball.
- Player B stands facing down the field.
- Player B passes to player C, who has first checked away and then checked back again.
- Player D checks away and checks back again to receive a pass from player C.
- D crosses to the incoming player E.
- Player E runs toward the near post and tries to score.
- The players must communicate.
- Circulation: A-B-C-D-E-F-G-H-A clockwise.

- Improving passing and kicking technique.

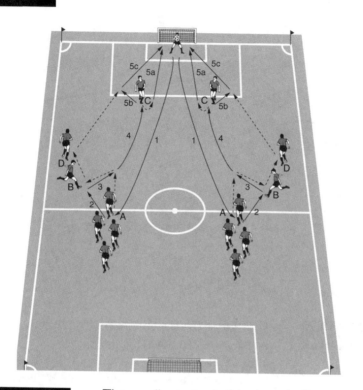

**ORGANIZATION:**
- The goalkeeper plays a long ball to player A.
- Player A plays a 1-2 combination with player B.
- Player A passes to striker C.
- Player D (makes a forward run to support player C.
- Player C or player D tries to score.

**INSTRUCTIONS:**
- Focus on passing.
- Play the ball to the correct foot (or just in front of the receiving player).

# PASSING

**OBJECTIVE:** Improving passing.

**ORGANIZATION:**
- One large fixed goal (in the penalty area) and two small portable goals.
- Sufficient balls (20).
- All positions are occupied by two players, so that the play can alternate over right and left.
- The coach passes to one of the two wingers. The ball can be played to the player's feet, or just in front of him, or well in front of him. The player makes a run to the end line and crosses the ball.
- The other three players have taken up positions in front of the goal.

**INSTRUCTIONS:**
- Stand ready to receive the ball, with your weight on the front of your foot.
- Choose between controlling the ball with your first touch, or pushing it in the direction you want to run, so that you can get away from your marker.
- Look up so that you can see the positions of the players in front of the goal.
- Decide what sort of cross to deliver.

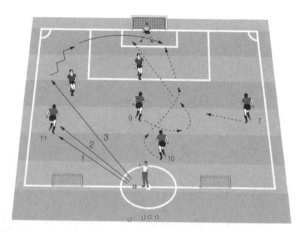

**OBJECTIVE:** Improving passing under pressure.

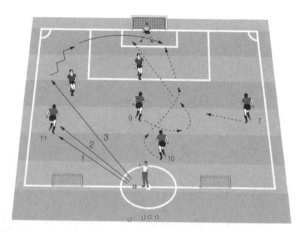

**ORGANIZATION:**
- One large fixed goal (in the penalty area) and two small portable goals.
- Sufficient balls (20).
- With two defenders; one defends in front of the goal and the other plays as a full back.
- The winger creates space by checking away and then back again.
- The full back can mark the winger more closely, leaving space behind him for a pass into the winger's path, or he can stand off the winger, who can then receive a pass to his feet and make a run down the flank.
- The other defender tries to defend against the players in front of the goal.
- If the defenders or the goalkeeper gain possession, they must try to score in a small goal (long shot).

**INSTRUCTIONS:**
- Decide what sort of cross to make (high, low, hard or looping).
- You don't always have to reach the end line in order to deliver a good cross.

# PASSING

**OBJECTIVE:** Small sided game of 6v6 with 3 neutral players in one zone and a striker (lay-off player) in the other

**ORGANIZATION:**
- The team with the ball play it around freely at first, then the players are limited to 2-touch play. The lay-off players are only allowed two touches.
- A long forward pass is only allowed after the ball has been played back (cooperation between lay-off player 9 and 10).
- A diagonal pass to the player making the forward run scores points.
- One team of six tries to keep possession in one zone. 1 point is awarded for 10 successive passes.
- If the ball goes out of play, the team in possession keeps the ball, but starts again with 0 points.

- The other team must try to intercept the ball. It scores points if one of its players makes a forward pass and a support run to receive the lay-off from the striker. Two points are awarded for a good 1-2 combination with the striker.
- Before the forward pass is delivered, each team always plays toward the same end and keeps possession in the same zone.

**INSTRUCTIONS:**
- Press properly, work together.
- Positions after winning possession.
- Who makes the forward run, and when?
- Lay-off players on the flank go with the play to the other zone.

# SHOOTING

**OBJECTIVE:** Improving ball control and final run.

**ORGANIZATION:**
- Finishing drill with 2 focal aspects (ball control and final run).
- Slalom down the center and try to score in a goal defended by a goalkeeper.

**INSTRUCTIONS:**
Ball control:
- Dribble/slalom using both feet.
- Play in firmly to the foot furthest away.
- Stand at an angle to the path of the ball for a firm long kick.

Final pass/final run:
- Estimate direction of run/speed of run by striker.
- Firm or short, slow it down.
- Play it square to the receiver.
- Call for the ball.
- Control the ball or take it immediately.
- Observe at the goalkeeper's position and area.

**OBJECTIVE:** Improving finishing with the weaker and stronger foot.

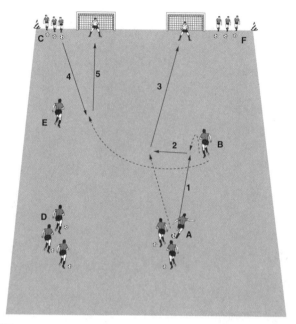

**ORGANIZATION:**
- Two large goals on the end line.
- 2 goalkeepers and 14 field players.
- Player B checks away and then checks back to receive a pass from player A.
- Player B plays the ball square and player A shoots at goal.
- Player B runs round the back of player A and receives a cross from player C in front of the other goal.
- Player B shoots at goal.
- It is then the turn of players D, E and F.
- The players always move to the next position.

**INSTRUCTIONS:**
- Pass to the correct foot.
- Correct shooting posture (especially when shooting with the weaker foot).
- Concentration.
- Correct speed; gradually work up to the fastest possible speed.

# SHOOTING

**OBJECTIVE:** Improving finishing.

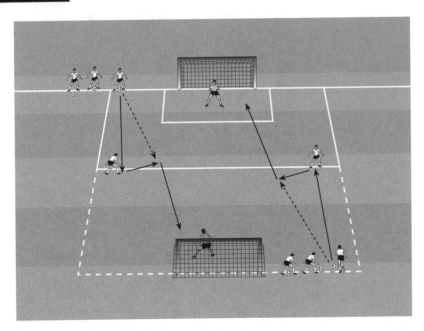

**ORGANIZATION:**
- Playing area: Twice the size of the penalty area; 2 large goals.
- Two groups with the same number of players.
- One player from each team stands in the field and the others stand on the end lines beside the goals.

**INSTRUCTIONS:**
- 1-2 combination play and shot a goal.
- Volley after a medium-high cross.
- 5v5 with two goals.
- One goal is defended by a goalkeeper. Only headed goals count in the other one.
- One team attacks the defended goal and one attacks the empty goal. The teams repeatedly swap roles.

# SHOOTING

**OBJECTIVE:** Improving finishing.

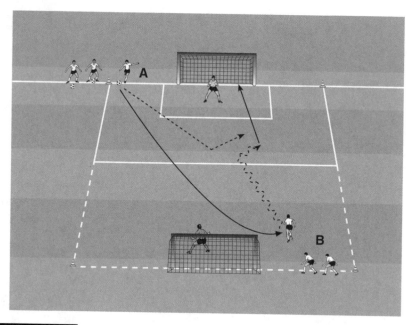

**ORGANIZATION:** Player A passes through the air to player B, who controls the ball and shoots at goal. The players then swap roles.

**INSTRUCTIONS:**
- After passing, player A becomes a defender (1v1).
- After the pass, two players become defenders (2v2).
- 2x5 minutes of 5v5 with goalkeepers, then 10 minutes of soccer tennis. -After passing, player A becomes a defender (1v1).

# SHOOTING

**OBJECTIVE:** Improving speed.

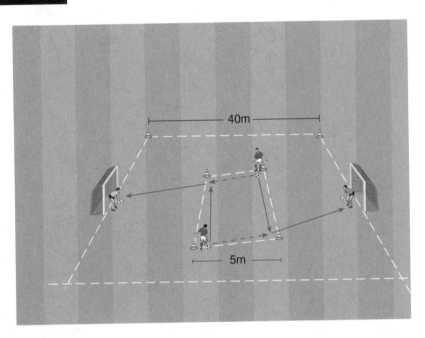

**ORGANIZATION:**
- Players A and B stand beside diagonally opposite cones, each with a ball at his feet.
- At a signal from the coach, each of them passes the ball across the face of the goal.
- Each player runs onto the other player's pass and shoots at goal.

**INSTRUCTIONS:** Pass the ball with a lot of pace, so that the other player has to sprint to reach it in time.

# SHOOTING

Improving speed.

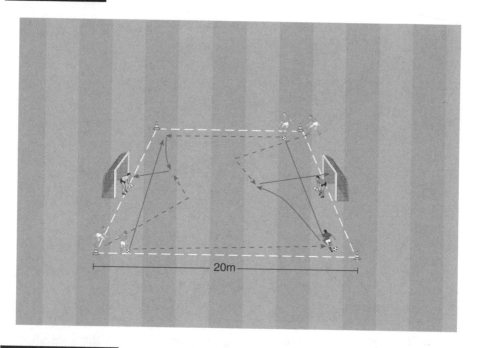

20m

**ORGANIZATION:**
- Two goals facing each other 20 yards apart, each of them defended by a goalkeeper.
- 10 yards to the right and left of each goal are cones, where the drill starts.
- Two players stand at each of two diagonally opposite cones.

**INSTRUCTIONS:**
- One player at each cone plays the ball straight across the goal, then sprints down the side line to meet the other player's pass and cross it back in front of the goal.
- The second player at each cone runs into the middle to meet the cross and tries to score.

# SHOOTING

**OBJECTIVE:**
- Improving receiving and running with the ball.
- Improving finishing.

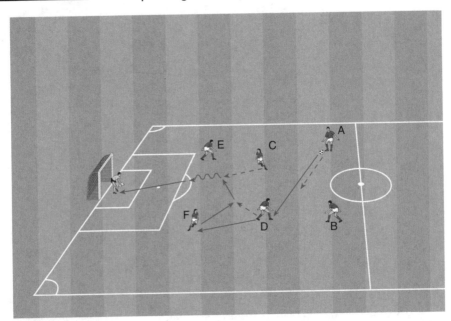

**ORGANIZATION:**
- In one half of a full sized pitch, two players stand beside the cones in front of the goal, which is defended by a goalkeeper.
- The other players stand with a ball at their feet on the left and right of the center circle.
- There are two cones on the left and right in front of the penalty area.

**INSTRUCTIONS:**
- The first player passes diagonally to the other player and runs after the ball.
- The other player controls the ball and turns towards the goal in one movement. He runs with the ball toward the goal, makes a fake movement in front of the cone and shoots at goal.

Variation
- Introduce defenders instead of cones.
- The attacker must try to beat the defender and then score.

Improving finishing from a 2 against 1 situation.

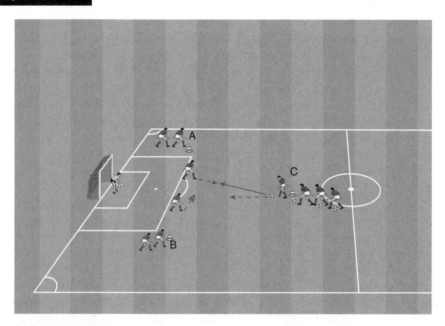

**ORGANIZATION:**
- The players are divided into three equal groups and take up their position in one half of a full sized pitch.
- Groups A and B are positioned at the right and left of the penalty area.
- Group C has the ball and is positioned beside the center circle.

**INSTRUCTIONS:**
- A player in group C passes to a player in group A and the two play 2 against 1 against one of the players from group B.
- After a goal is scored, each player moves on to the next group.

Variation
As above, but a second defender joins in from the end line to create a 2 against 2 situation (after the third pass; after 3 ball contacts; after the first pass; at a sign from the coach).

# SHOOTING

Improving finishing from a cross.

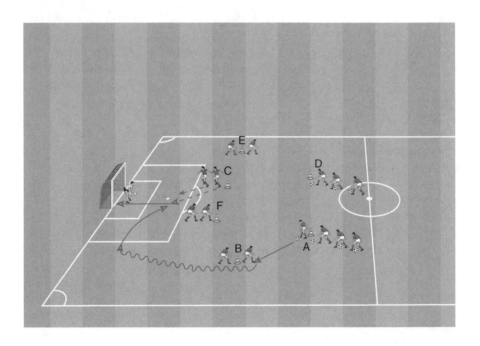

**ORGANIZATION:** 6 groups of players (A-F) distributed over one half of a full sized pitch. Goal defended by goalkeeper.

**INSTRUCTIONS:**
- A player from group A passes to a player from group B, who makes a forward run with the ball toward the end line and crosses to a player from group C.
- The attacker from group C is accompanied by a defender as he runs toward the penalty area and tries to score.
- A player from group D starts the next sequence from the other side with a pass to a player from group E, who crosses to a player from group F, etc.

# SHOOTING

**OBJECTIVE:**  Improving finishing from fixed positions.

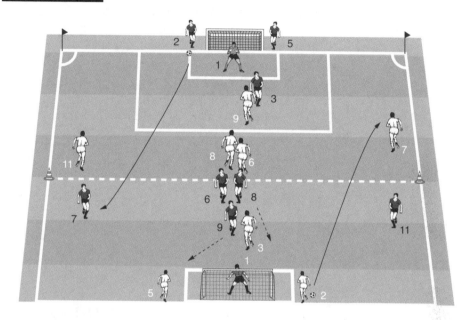

**ORGANIZATION:**
- Everyone starts from his own position.
- 2 full backs from behind the goal, 2 wingers, 1 striker and one "hanging" player behind the striker.
- Two players fill the "hanging" position behind the striker, as this position requires a lot of running.
- A central defender marks the striker closely.
- The sequence is carried out on each flank in opposite directions, and is started by the full backs.
- Each full back raises an arm to signal the start, and the two simultaneously play a long pass to the winger.
- The defender at the other side of the goal then moves forward from the end line.

- The first pass must be played firmly.
- Winger controls the ball and moves inside.
- In front of the goal, the striker determines when and where the "hanging" player runs into space.
- Player 2 plays the ball to player 7, who controls it and crosses.
- In front of goal, player 9 combines with player 8 or player 6 to create a 2 against 1 advantage against player 3.
- After player 2 plays the ball to player 7 he moves into the center in front of his own goal, thus creating a 2 against 2 situation.
- The winger can also try to score!

# SHOOTING

**50**

**OBJECTIVE:** Improving finishing from fixed positions.

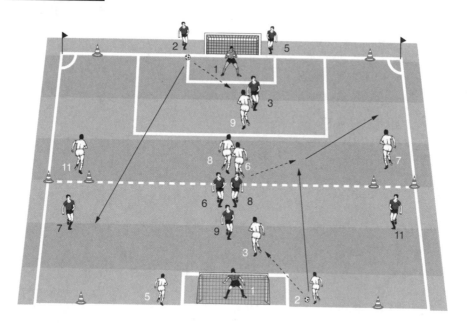

**ORGANIZATION:**
- Everyone starts from his own position.
- 2 full backs from behind the goal, 2 wingers, 1 striker and one "hanging" player behind the striker.
- Two players fill the "hanging" position behind the striker, as this position requires a lot of running.
- A central defender marks the striker closely.
- The sequence is carried out on each flank in opposite directions, and is started by the full backs.
- Each full back raises an arm to signal the start, and the two simultaneously play a long pass to the winger.
- The defender at the other side of the goal then moves forward from the end line.

- The first pass must be played firmly.
- Winger controls the ball and moves inside.
- In front of the goal, the striker determines when and where the "hanging" player runs into space.
- The ball is played first to player 6, who controls it and plays it into the path of player 7. Player 11 moves into the middle, creating a 3 against 2 situation in front of the goal.

# SHOOTING 51

Improving finishing from fixed positions.

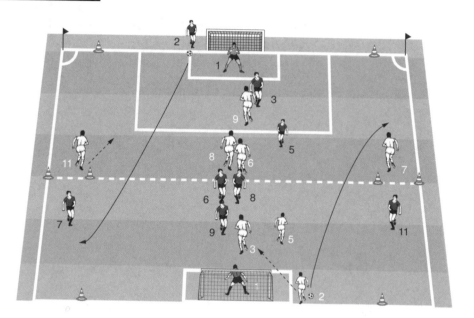

**ORGANIZATION:**

- Everyone starts from his own position.
- 2 full backs from behind the goal, 2 wingers, 1 striker and one "hanging" player behind the striker.
- Two players fill the "hanging" position behind the striker, as this position requires a lot of running.
- A central defender marks the striker closely.
- The sequence is carried out on each flank in opposite directions, and is started by the full backs.
- Each full back raises an arm to signal the start, and the two simultaneously play a long pass to the winger.
- The defender at the other side of the goal then moves forward from the end line.

- The first pass must be played firmly.
- Winger controls the ball and moves inside.
- In front of the goal, the striker determines when and where the "hanging" player runs into space.
- Player 5 or player 2 marks position 10.
- The passer now plays the ball directly to the winger.
- The player behind the goal passes the ball from the left as well as the right.
- There is now a 4 against 3 situation in front of the goal.

Improving build-up play down the flanks.

**ORGANIZATION:**

- Player 4 passes the ball to the feet of player 7 (who first checks away and then checks back to create space). Player 7 takes the ball and runs at the full back.
- Player 4 passes the ball forward.
- Player 3 passes the ball to player to player 11 (who first checks away and then checks back to create space), who gets past his marker by playing a 1-2 combination with player 8.

**INSTRUCTIONS:**

- Fake and eye contact between players 7 and 4, and 3 and 11.
- Timing of player 8's move to play the 1-2 combination.
- Play the ball to the correct foot.

# COMBINATION PLAY

**OBJECTIVE:**  Improving build-up play down the flanks.

**ORGANIZATION:**
- Player 4 passes the ball to the feet of player 7, who first checks away and then checks back to create space.
- Player 7 takes the ball and runs at the defender. Player 6 makes an overlap run down the flank.
- Player 5 passes the ball to player 11, who passes it first time to 9.

**INSTRUCTIONS:**
- 2 against 1 situation, so players 7 and 6 have to work together.
- Player 9 has to anticipate what player 11 will do in situations where player 11 has a defender close behind him.
- The pass from player 5 to player 11 is usually a poor option, as player 11 is closely marked and can only pass the ball back to player 5.

**OBJECTIVE:**

Improving fixed attacking moves.

**ORGANIZATION:**

- Everyone in his own position.
- Alternate over right and left.
- Central defender plays a 1-2 combination with the central midfielder.
- Pass out to the winger.
- Play the ball back to the full back.
- The full back plays a forward pass for the midfielder to run onto.
- The midfielder overlaps and crosses for the two strikers.
- Midfielder and full back keep moving.
- The two strikers cross as they run in at the goal and try to score.
- The scoring attempt is followed by a stoppable shot at the goalkeeper.

**INSTRUCTIONS:**

- Concentration and accuracy are required.
- Diagonal pass or pass down the side line to the player who has to cross the ball.
- The goalkeeper must react immediately to the second shot after the first one.

Improving fixed attacking moves.

**ORGANIZATION:**

- Everyone in his own position, but now only six players (the other players play 5v2 in a small zone at the edge of the playing area).
- Alternate over right and left.
- Central defender plays a 1-2 combination with the central defender.
- Play the out to the winger.
- Winger makes a run to the end line and crosses.
- The two strikers cross as they run at goal and try to score.
- The scoring attempt is followed by a stoppable shot at the goalkeeper.

**INSTRUCTIONS:**

- Concentration and accuracy are required.
- The ball must be played into the path of the winger.
- The winger must pay close attention to the situation in front of the goal.
- The goalkeeper must react immediately to the second shot after the first one.

# COMBINATION PLAY   56

Improving play down the flanks.

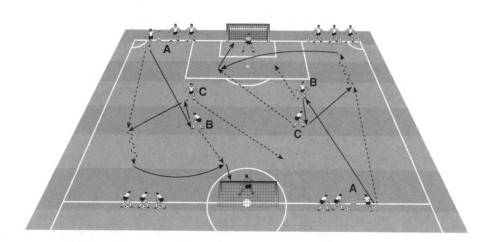

**ORGANIZATION:**
- One half of a full sized pitch; 2 goals defended by goalkeepers.
- Each team has 2 wingers (B and C).
- The other players are divided evenly over the four corners of the playing area.
- The two diagonally opposite groups start the drill simultaneously.

**INSTRUCTIONS:**
- Player A crosses to player B, who volleys it to his teammate C.
- Player C plays a firm first-time pass to the feet of player A, who is making a fast run down the flank.
- Player A takes the ball forward and crosses to incoming player B or C, who tries to volley or head it into the goal.
- After each 5 plays: switch the attacking positions.

Improving 1 against 1 skills.

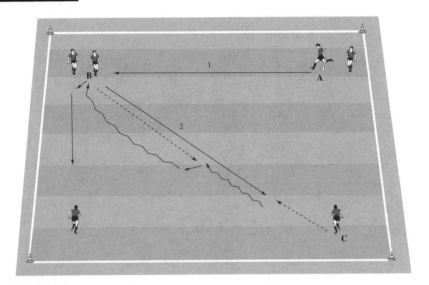

**ORGANIZATION:**
- Square measuring 10x10 yards.
- Six players.
- One ball.

**INSTRUCTIONS:**
- Firm pass from A to B.
- B plays first-time diagonal pass to C and runs after the ball toward C.
- C comes to meet the ball, controls it and tries to take it past B (fake).
- C continues his run with the ball until he reaches the opposite corner, then passes the ball along the side line.
- The sequence is then repeated along the other diagonal.

Coaching (defenders)
- Keep low.
- Don't challenge your opponent from the front but force him to one side.
- Neutralize your opponent's speed.
- Make contact with your opponent.

**OBJECTIVE:** Improving 1 against 1 skills.

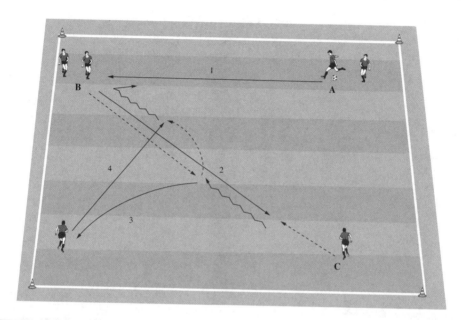

**ORGANIZATION:**
- Square measuring 10x10 yards.
- Six players.
- One ball.
- The player with the ball can also make use of a 1-2 combination.

**INSTRUCTIONS:**
- Make contact quickly with your opponent, reduce his options.
- Force your opponent to make mistakes.
- Don't approach your opponent from the front. Try to neutralize his stronger foot.
- Don't get too close to your opponent, otherwise he will go past you.
- Step forward (back) when your opponent plays a 1-2 combination.
- Don't put your weight on your heels, as you will not be able to react quickly.

**OBJECTIVE:** Improving 1 against 1 skills.

**ORGANIZATION:**
- Three attackers on the edge of the penalty area, who keep moving to the next position.
- Three defenders stand beside the goal area with out a ball.

**INSTRUCTIONS:**
- The ball is played to the attacker standing beside the penalty area, who tries to get in front of goal.
- The defender challenges from the side and tries to prevent the attacker from scoring.
- Don't allow the attacker to turn and set up a frontal 1 against 1 situation.
- Get close to the attacker to block the ball. Take care with the final long stride, as the attacker might shoot between your legs (the goalkeeper will be taken by surprise).
- Use a well timed shoulder charge.
- Use a sliding tackle as a last resort.

Improving 1 against 1 skills.

**ORGANIZATION:**
- Three attackers on the edge of the penalty area, who keep moving to the next position.
- Three defenders stand beside the goal area with out a ball.

**INSTRUCTIONS:**
- The ball is played to the attacker standing beside the penalty area, who tries to get in front of goal.
- The defender challenges from the side and tries to prevent the attacker from scoring.
- Don't allow the attacker to turn and set up a frontal 1 against 1 situation.
- Get close to the attacker to block the ball. Take care with the final long stride, as the attacker might shoot between your legs (the goalkeeper will be taken by surprise).
- Use a well timed shoulder charge.
- Use a sliding tackle as a last resort.

**OBJECTIVE:**

Improving 1 against 1 skills as an attacker faced with a defender in the center of the field, in combination with passing and shooting at a goal defended by a goalkeeper.

**ORGANIZATION:**

- Two defenders on each side of the goal.
- Large goal defended by goalkeeper.
- Four attackers distributed across the center line.
- The balls are on the end line.

**INSTRUCTIONS:**

- A defender kicks a ball from the end line towards a winger.
- The winger passes square into the middle.
- The attacker runs with the ball toward the defender and tries to score.
- The defenders move through to the next position.
- The defenders score by winning the ball and then making a forward pass or a pass back to the goalkeeper.
- Play on both the right and the left flank.
- The key aspect of the game is the 1 against 1 situation in the center.

Improving 1 against 1 skills of attackers and defenders

**ORGANIZATION:**
-4 defenders, 4 attackers, 1 goalkeeper.
-1 large goal and two small goals.

**INSTRUCTIONS:**

- A defender kicks the ball to an attacker and pressures the attacker; in this phase the attacker and defender work with less than maximum pressure and resistance, preparing to build up to a maximum.
- A defender kicks the ball to an attacker and exerts maximum pressure.
- Defenders: Move up quickly towards the attackers, keeping your knees bent.
- Use fakes to trick the attacker into choosing the wrong moment to try to take the ball past you.
- Use your body when your opponent is not quite past you.
- Decide what is the correct moment to exert pressure or try to win the ball. This often depends on the position of the attacker as well as the defender.

**OBJECTIVE:**
- Improving strength in 1 against 1 situations.
- Improving repeated short sprint capacity.

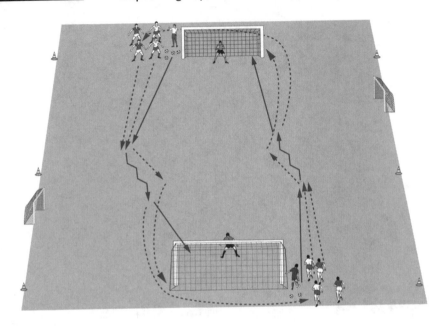

**ORGANIZATION:**
- Number of players: 8 plus 2 permanent goalkeepers.
- Playing area: The size of 2 penalty areas.
- Beside each large goal is one neutral player (e.g. the assistant coach) who plays the balls into the field.
- Two pairs of players, each consisting of one defender and one attacker, stand beside each neutral player.

**INSTRUCTIONS:**
- The neutral player plays a ball into the field every five seconds.
- An attacker and a defender sprint to the ball.
- If the attacker wins, he tries to score in the other goal.
- If the defender wins, he scores in one of the small goals on the side lines. This symbolizes clearing the ball quickly and calmly down the flanks.
- After each duel, each pair of players has 10 seconds to join a pair of players at the other end.
- For each pair, a series initially consists of 6 sprints.

**OBJECTIVE:**
- Improving efficiency when in possession by:
  - shielding the ball;
  - being aware of what is happening around the ball;
  - efficient use of the body.

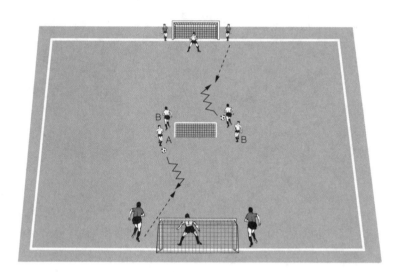

**ORGANIZATION:**
- Player A starts: 1 against 1 with defender; then player B starts: 1 against 1 with defender.
- The attacker scores in the large goal and the defender scores in the net.
- Move to the next position: the defender always swaps places with the defender.
- After a series of 4, player A swaps with player B.

**INSTRUCTIONS:**
- Keep your weight on the front of your feet, so you can react more quickly.
- Stand at an angle to the path of the ball, feet pointing outward; you can then turn faster.
- Knees slightly bent, stay low.
- Don't snatch at the ball.
- Stay on your feet; if you go to the ground, you take yourself out of the play.

**OBJECTIVE:**
- Improving efficiency when in possession by:
  - shielding the ball;
  - being aware of what is happening around the ball;
  - efficient use of the body.

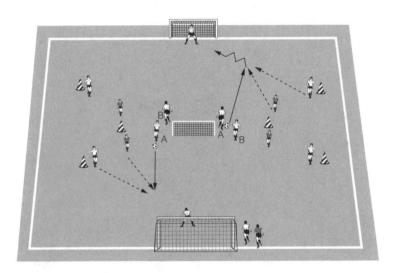

**ORGANIZATION:**
- Player A starts: he plays the ball to the winger; 1 against 1 with defender; then player B starts.
- Move to the next position: player A becomes a defender, the defender becomes a winger, the winger goes to the position of player A.
- After a series of 4, player A swaps with player B.

**INSTRUCTIONS:**
- Try to get in front of your opponent.
- Disturb his run by cutting across in front of him.
- Tense your body, make your body (shoulders!) a block.
- Try to set your shoulder against your opponent's shoulder.
- Get involved in the situation, but don't commit any fouls.
- A tackle is a last resort: if you go to the ground, you take yourself out of the play.

- Improving efficiency when in possession by:
  - shielding the ball;
  - being aware of what is happening around the ball;
  - efficient use of the body.

- Player A starts: he plays the ball to the winger; 1 against 1 with defender; then player B starts.
- Each player moves through to the next position: player A becomes a defender, the defender becomes a winger, the winger goes to the position of player A.
- After the sequence has been carried out 4 times, player A swaps with player B.

- Stand at an angle to your opponent – you can get forward quicker.
- Try to get in front of your opponent.
- Make sure your opponent knows you are there.
- Stay on your feet.
- Mark closely: give him no space.
- Make sure that you are 'in contact' with your opponent.

Improving 1 against 1 skills (attackers).

**ORGANIZATION:**
- Large goal defended by goalkeeper.
- Large undefended goal on the edge of the center circle.
- Defender starts on the edge of the penalty area.
- Attacker starts just over the edge of the center circle.

**INSTRUCTIONS:**
- Player A passes to player B.
- Player B passes to player C.
- Player C tries to take the ball past player B.
- Player C tries to score in the large goal defended by a goalkeeper.
- Player B tries to prevent player C from scoring; after winning possession, he tries to score in the goal beside the center circle.
- Move through to the next position: A-B, B-C, C-A. Or work specifically with attackers and defenders.

**OBJECTIVE:** Improving 1 against 1 skills (attackers).

**ORGANIZATION:**
- Large goal defended by goalkeeper.
- Large undefended goal on the edge of the center circle.
- Defender starts on the edge of the penalty area.
- Attacker starts just over the edge of the center circle.
- Balls on the center line, where the drill starts.

**INSTRUCTIONS:**
- Player B runs toward player A and calls for the ball.
- Player A passes to player B.
- Player B turns, taking the ball with him, and tries to take the ball past player C.
- Player C starts from the edge of the penalty area at the moment when the ball is played to player B.
- Player B tries to score in the large goal defended by a goalkeeper.
- Player C tries to prevent player B from scoring, and after winning possession he tries to score in the goal beside the center circle.
- Move through to the next position: A-B, B-C, C-A. Or work specifically with attackers and defenders.

Improving 1 against 1 skills (attackers).

**ORGANIZATION:**
- Slightly more than a quarter of a full sized pitch.
- Large goal defended by a goalkeeper.
- Two junior goals at the positions on the sides where the attackers start from.
- Sufficient balls beside the junior goals.
- The first ball is played from the edge of the center circle.

**INSTRUCTIONS:**
- The winger receives a long pass from the center of the field.
- As soon as he controls the ball, the defender can challenge him.
- What the defender decides to do depends on the winger's run (how he receives and runs with the ball, whether he has the ball under control or not).
- The attacker can go through the middle or down the flank.
- The defender tries to prevent the attacker from scoring or crossing the ball; if he wins the ball he can score in the goal beside the side line.

# SMALL SIDED GAMES (1V1)

**OBJECTIVE:** Improving 1 against 1 skills (defenders).

**ORGANIZATION:**
- Quarter of a full sized pitch.
- Large goal defended by a goalkeeper.
- Two junior goals at the positions on the side lines where the attackers start.
- Sufficient balls beside the junior goals.
- Two cones level with the edge of the goal area, 5 yards outside the penalty area.

**INSTRUCTIONS:**
- A winger starts about 25 yards from the end line with the ball at his foot.
- He must try to cross the ball.
- He cannot cross the ball until he goes past the cone on the outside.
- The defender starts just inside the end line and tries to prevent the attacker from crossing the ball.
- After the defender wins the ball, he can score in the goal near the side line.

**OBJECTIVE:** Improving the use of the switch pass.

**ORGANIZATION:**
- Half of a full sized pitch.
- Sufficient balls half way down the field outside the side line.
- Goal defended by a goalkeeper.
- The positions of the wingers and midfielders are doubly occupied.

**INSTRUCTIONS:**
- Finishing drill without any resistance, to practice routine moves.
- The left winger makes a short run with the ball (in any direction).
- One of the two central midfielders runs into space and receives a pass from the winger. He lays it off to another midfielder who moves up from behind him.
- The second midfielder plays a crossfield pass (switch pass) to the right wing.
- The winger takes the ball on the run at speed. He crosses for the two incoming players.

**OBJECTIVE:**    Improving individual defending technique (frontal).

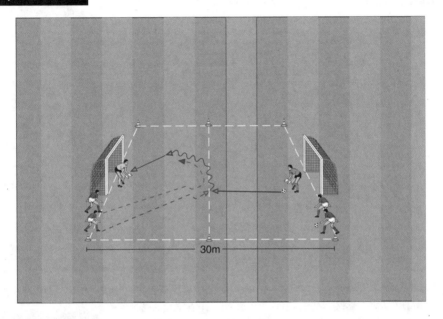

30m

**ORGANIZATION:**    Two goals 20 yards apart, both defended by goal-keepers.

**INSTRUCTIONS:**

- Player C plays the ball into the path of player A, who sprints to the ball and tries to score in the goal behind player C.
- Player B tries to prevent player C from scoring. If player B wins the ball, he tries to score in the other goal.
- Always watch the ball and your opponent.
- Be alert, always be ready to react to your opponent's every move.
- Adjust to the speed and direction of the attacker's run.
- Wait for the right moment to win the ball.
- Don't dive in.

Variation
Goalkeeper C plays the ball through the air to player A.

**OBJECTIVE:**

Improving individual defending technique (opponent behind defender's back).

**ORGANIZATION:**

- Use cones to mark a playing area of 20 by 30 yards, divided into three zones.
- Goal, defended by goalkeeper, 15 yards behind each end line.
- Three players in each zone.

**INSTRUCTIONS:**

- The players in zone 1 try to hit a firm pass to a teammate in zone 3. If this succeeds, the receiving player tries to score.
- The players in the middle zone try to position themselves correctly so that they can intercept the ball. If a player intercepts a pass, he tries to dribble past the player who made the pass (1 against 1) and score a goal.
- Unless the attacker plays the ball too far ahead, the defender in a 1 against 1 situation should wait for the right moment to try to win the ball (without committing a foul).
- In a 1 against 1 situation, the defender should try to stay at the ideal distance from the attacker (no bodily contact, but close enough to try to win the ball at any moment).

# SMALL SIDED GAMES (1V2) 74

Improving defending technique.

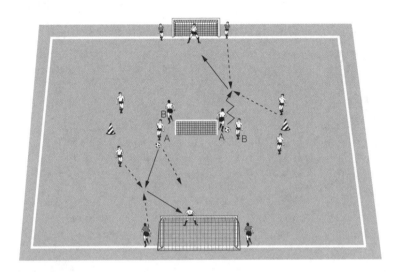

**ORGANIZATION:**
- Two attackers against 1 defender and a goalkeeper.
- The 2 attackers try to score in the large goal. The defender and the goalkeeper can score in the net.
- The players move to the next position. Player A becomes the defender, the defender becomes the winger, the winger goes to the position of player A.
- After carrying out the drill four times, player A and player B swap roles.
- Success: when the defender and the goalkeeper score, attackers have to carry out additional work!

**INSTRUCTIONS:**
- Work together with the goalkeeper.
- Take up defending position between the two attackers. Force the attackers to make a choice.

**OBJECTIVE:**   Link-up by third man.

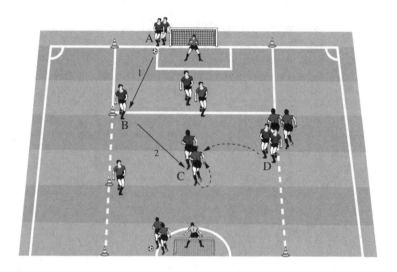

**ORGANIZATION:**
- Half of a full sized pitch.
- Extension of the penalty area.
- Two large goals.
- 14 players and 2 goalkeepers.

**INSTRUCTIONS:**
- 2v1 situation in front of the goal.
- Start alternately.
- Attackers score in large goal.
- Start at the other end when a goal is scored or the defender wins the ball.
- Defender A plays the ball to midfielder B.
- Midfielder B plays the ball to attacker C.
- Winger (or withdrawn striker) D joins in.
- Then 2 against 1.

**OBJECTIVE:**
- Switching flanks.
- Positions in front of goal and finishing.

**ORGANIZATION:**
- Half of a full sized pitch.
- One large goal.
- 20 players and 3 goalkeepers.

**INSTRUCTIONS:**
- Get the ball into space by switching flanks.
- Cross and finish.
- 2 attackers and 1 defender in front of the goal.
- 3 attackers and 2 defenders in front of the goal.
- Attackers score in large goal.
- Start on the other side after a goal is scored or after the defenders win the ball.

**OBJECTIVE:**   Improving crossing the ball.

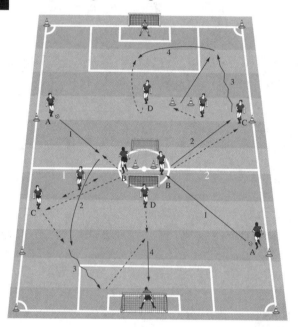

**ORGANIZATION:**
- Work in two directions.
- A plays the ball to B.
- B turns and plays the ball to winger C.
- 2 against 1 + goalkeeper (winger and striker against defender and goalkeeper).
- Attackers score in large goal and defenders in small goal.

**INSTRUCTIONS:**

Winger (C)
- Check away and check back to create space.
- Make sure you are available to take a pass.
- Take the ball with the outside of your foot.
- A forward pass is the preferred option.
- Stay in touch with the player in front of the goal.

The central player (B)
- Adjust the speed of the ball.
- Communicate with the winger.
- Make sure the ball is immediately playable.

The full back (A)
- Play the ball to the central player in such a way that he can easily control it.
- Adjust the speed of the ball.

The striker (D)
- Don't run in at the goal too quickly – make sure that are available to receive a pass.

**OBJECTIVE:** Improving 2 against 2 play.

**ORGANIZATION:**

- Two of the three defenders who start in the goal area always work together.
- Two of the three attackers who start outside the penalty area always work together.

**INSTRUCTIONS:**

- The defenders play the ball to the attackers.
- The attackers try to score as quickly as possible.
- The defenders try to prevent this in cooperation with the goalkeeper.
- The goalkeeper must communicate with his defenders.
- The last man must communicate with his teammate.
- Let your teammates know where you are, and cover their backs.

**OBJECTIVE:**    Improve 1 against 1 play.

**ORGANIZATION:**
- Two defenders and a goalkeeper.
- Two attackers.
- The ball is played to the midfielder, who must cooperate with the winger to try and score.
- 2 against 2.
- Defenders: cut out the cross or the inside run?

**INSTRUCTIONS:**
- Communicate with each other. The front man is reassured by your communication and gains in confidence. Short and clear communications.
- Force your opponent to play the ball back.
- If the attacker stops and plays the ball back, that is the moment to make a determined attempt to win the ball.

**OBJECTIVE:**    Improving defensive play.

**ORGANIZATION:**
- 2 against 2 situations.
- Two large goals defended by goalkeepers.
- Two teams of 6 players.

**INSTRUCTIONS:**
- Two attackers from the blue team try to score against two defenders from the red team.
- If the defenders win the ball, they try to score.
- After a maximum of 1 minute, switch.
- The offside rule applies.

# SMALL SIDED GAMES (2v2)

Improving ball-oriented defensive play.

**ORGANIZATION:**
- 2 against 2 situations.
- Two teams of six players.

**INSTRUCTIONS:**
- The two defenders try to prevent the attackers from crossing the line with the ball.
- Both teams try to score. A goal is scored when a player runs between the cones with the ball at his feet.
- The team that scores keeps possession of the ball and faces new opponents.

<table>
<tr><td>**OBJECTIVE:**</td><td>Improving ball-oriented defensive play.</td></tr>
</table>

<table>
<tr><td>**ORGANIZATION:**</td><td>- 2 against 2 situations.<br>- Two teams of six players.</td></tr>
</table>

<table>
<tr><td>**INSTRUCTIONS:**</td><td>- Striker B calls for the ball.<br>- Player A passes to player B.<br>- Players A and B try to score in the large goal.<br>- If the defenders win the ball, they can score (one of them has to run between the cones with the ball at his feet).</td></tr>
</table>

**OBJECTIVE:** Improving ball-oriented defensive play.

**ORGANIZATION:**
- 2 against 2 situations.
- Two teams of six players.

**INSTRUCTIONS:**
- Striker E calls for the ball.
- Player A and player B play the first pass alternately.
- The player with the ball decides whether to pass or run with the ball at his feet.

**OBJECTIVE:** Improving the final pass and final run.

**ORGANIZATION:**
- Positional game before final pass or final run.
- A runs forward with ball, keeping his eye on B.
- B runs into space to receive a pass from A.
- With his first touch, B passes the ball square to C, who has checked away and checks back to receive the pass.
- C runs forward with the ball at his feet and chooses to pass either to D (striker) or E (midfielder).
- D is covered by a defender close behind him.
- At the moment when B plays the ball to C, E can start to defend. This creates a 2 against 2 situation.
- The 2 attackers must try to score in the large goal.
- The defenders must play the ball out of defense and score in the small goal as quickly as possible (within 10 seconds). The goalkeeper plays on the defender's side and can therefore join in.

**INSTRUCTIONS:**
Attackers
- Get ready for the pass to the midfielder (B).
- The striker (D) and midfielder (E) must choose where to stand relative to each other: get forward or get behind the ball.
- After losing possession, exert pressure; prevent the ball from being played forward, and communicate with each other.

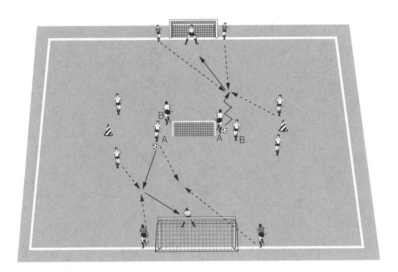

# SMALL SIDED GAMES (2v2)   **85**

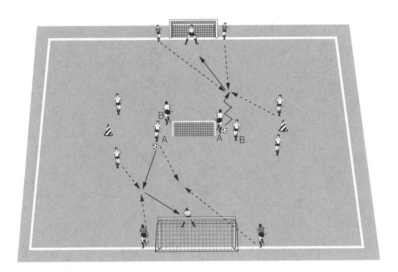

**OBJECTIVE:** Improving cooperation between defender and goalkeeper.

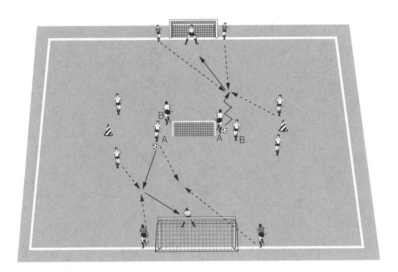

**ORGANIZATION:**
- This game promotes cooperation between the defender and the goalkeeper.
- 2 against 2.
- Each player moves through to the next position after a goal is scored. The attackers become defenders and vice versa.
- Success: When the attackers score, the defenders remain where they are!

**INSTRUCTIONS:**
- Cover each other (help).
- Communicate with each other.

**OBJECTIVE:**  Improving defending.

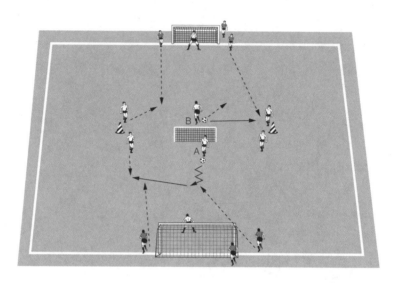

**ORGANIZATION:**

- An important aspect of this game is that the two defenders have to push toward the side where the ball is.
- Each player moves through to the next position: the attackers become defenders and vice versa: 1 defender can always recuperate.
- Success: When the attackers score, the defenders remain where they are!

**INSTRUCTIONS:**

- Cooperation with the goalkeeper.
- Cover each other (help).
- Communicate with each other.

**OBJECTIVE:**   Improving ball-oriented defensive play.

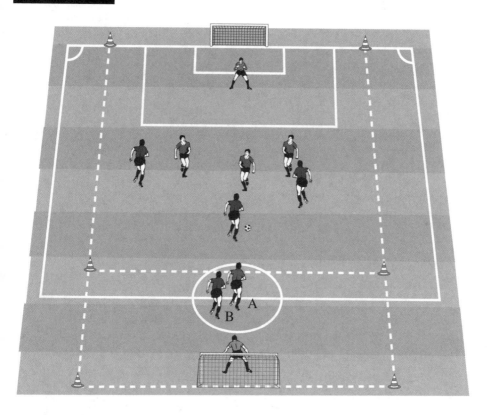

**ORGANIZATION:**
- Game of 3+1+goalkeeper v 3+1+goalkeeper.
- Two teams of four players plus a goalkeeper.

**INSTRUCTIONS:**
- The attacking team (blue) tries to score from the 3 against 3 situation.
- If the defending team (red) wins the ball, they try to play in their striker (A).
- Player A tries to win the 1 against 1 confrontation and score.
- If player B wins the ball from player A, he plays it to the attackers again.

**OBJECTIVE:**   Improving teamwork.

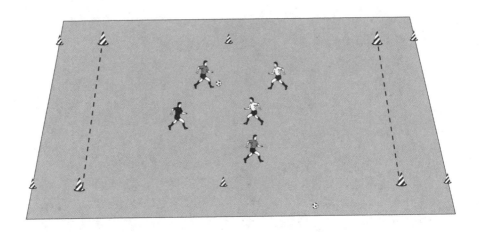

**ORGANIZATION:**
- Playing area 20 x 12 yards.
- End zone 12 x 2 yards.
- Six cones mark the extent of the playing area.
- Two small cones behind each end line mark a scoring zone 2 yards deep.
- One ball is in the playing area and a reserve ball is just outside the playing area.
- A total of 4 small cones, 6 larger cones, 2 balls and 3 vests are needed.

**INSTRUCTIONS:**
- The team with the ball tries to score by passing to each other until the can cross the opponent's end line and leave the ball in the scoring zone.
- The team with the ball starts off from its own end line.
- The neutral player always plays for the team that is in possession; he can also score.
- The winner is the first team to score three points.
- After about 5 minutes, the coach signals a change. The neutral player swaps with one of the others.
- If a player sends the ball out of the playing area, the other team gains possession and dribbles the ball back into play.

**OBJECTIVE:** Link-up by the third man.

**ORGANIZATION:**
- Half of a full sized pitch.
- Extension of the penalty area.
- Two large goals.
- 14 field players plus 2 goalkeepers.

**INSTRUCTIONS:**
- 3 against 2 situation in front of the goal.
- Game starts at the other end if a goal is scored or a defender wins the ball.
- Defender A plays the ball in to midfielder B.
- Midfielder B turns and plays the ball to striker C.
- Player B makes a forward run to support the striker.
- Winger (or withdrawn striker) D also makes a run forward.
- 1 defender near the goal chooses position.
- 3v2.
- All the players go back to their original positions.

**OBJECTIVE:** Practicing build-up play.

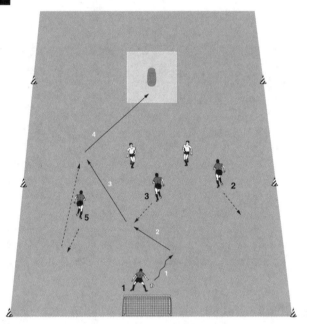

**ORGANIZATION:**
- Large playing area: 15 to 20 yards x 30 yards.
- The attackers score in the goal.
- The defenders score by shooting at an empty drum from outside the zone.
- The defenders must score 6 times to win, and the attackers must score 4 times.

**INSTRUCTIONS:**
The goalkeeper:
- Put the ball on the ground.
- Dribble the ball forward.
- Try to play your teammate into space.
- Join in when you do not have the ball yourself.
- Communicate, help your teammates! ('play it back', 'free', 'turn', etc.).

Players 2 and 5:
- Stand on the flank with your back to the side line.
- Check away from the ball and then check back to create space.
- Take the ball with the outside of your foot.

**OBJECTIVE:**    Finding space (midfielders).

**ORGANIZATION:**
- Three zones.
  - -3v2 in the first zone.
  - -2v2 in the second zone.
  - -2v3 in the third zone.

**INSTRUCTIONS:**
- Movement when the ball is worked into space in one of the two zones. Teammates in the furthest zone must anticipate the moment when a midfielder gains possession.
- Focus on the pass from the central defender, who plays the ball forward to the inside of the right midfielder.
- The midfielder checks away and checks back to create space to receive the ball, which he immediately plays to the striker if the striker has moved into space to receive the pass.
- The strikers in zone 3 must remain alert.

**OBJECTIVE:** Supporting an attacking move.

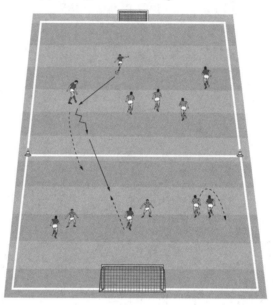

**ORGANIZATION:**

- Game of 3v3 in two zones. One player makes a forward run to support the strikers (4v3 in attacking zone).
- A player calls for the ball in the attacking zone of the team with the ball.
- The player who passes makes a forward run into the attacking zone to support the attack.
- The four attackers try to exploit their numerical advantage to score a goal.

**INSTRUCTIONS:**

- Timing of the call for the ball. The player with the ball must have the space to be able to pass.
- Play the ball forward correctly; the receiver must be able to lay the ball off to the player making the forward run.
- The four attackers must quickly adopt a good shape (diamond formation) in order to give themselves as much space as possible.
- The player who makes the forward pass and the forward run must communicate with his teammates because he has the best overview of the new situation.

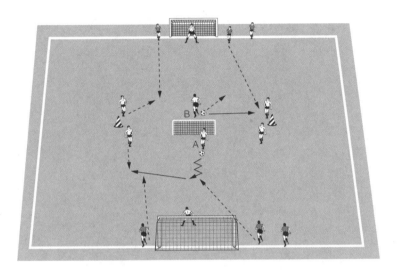

**OBJECTIVE:** Improving defensive play.

**ORGANIZATION:**
- The ideal drill for practicing one against one! Either let the players move to the next position after each goal, or choose a game drill that lasts for a given time.
- Success: The first player to score 3 goals remains an attacker!

**INSTRUCTIONS:**
- Help your teammate by pushing toward the flank where the ball is!
- Force your opponent away from the goal.

**OBJECTIVE:** Rapid ball circulation.

**ORGANIZATION:**
- Teams of 6 players.
- 3 players play in the defensive half and 3 in the attacking half.
- The offside rule applies.

**INSTRUCTIONS:**
- Play the ball to the striker. The third man must make a forward run.
- When you have a numerical advantage, keep the playing area a large as possible and try to play in the spare man.
- If you are at a numerical disadvantage, try to close down the available space.

# SMALL SIDED GAMES (3v3)

Improving defensive play.

**ORGANIZATION:**
- Game of 3v3.
- Two teams of six players.

**INSTRUCTIONS:**
- You can score by dribbling through one of the two lines with the ball at your feet.
- The three defenders try to prevent the attackers from dribbling over the line.
- The coaching focus is on defending correctly.
- If necessary, stop the play and explain the situation.

**ORGANIZATION:**
- Game of 3+keeper against 3.
- Two teams of six players, plus one goalkeeper.

**INSTRUCTIONS:**
- In the 3v3 confrontation, the blue team tries to score in the large goal defended by the goalkeeper.
- If the defending team (red) wins the ball, they try to pass to their strikers.
- The red team tries to score against the blue team by dribbling through one of the three zones.
- If the defenders win the ball, they play it to their strikers again.

**OBJECTIVE:**    Improving playing with three defenders in the final line.

**ORGANIZATION:**
- Half of a full sized pitch.
- Three defenders and three attackers.
- Goalkeeper in large goal.
- Small goal on the center spot.

**INSTRUCTIONS:**
- Three attackers start on the center line with a ball and try to score in the goal, which is defended by a goalkeeper.
- Three defenders start on the edge of the penalty area and try to prevent the attackers from scoring. If they win the ball they try to score in the small goal on the center line.
- The offside rule applies.
- No throw-ins or goal kicks; the play always starts with the three attackers.

**OBJECTIVE:**
- Improving passing technique.
- Improving the first and second touch when receiving a pass.

**ORGANIZATION:**
- Two teams of 8 players consisting of:
  two defenders,
  two defensive midfielders,
  one attacking midfielder,
  two wingers and one striker.

**INSTRUCTIONS:**
- Two teams play in one half of a full sized pitch with only one goal.
- In the middle zone, the teams play 3 against 3.
- On the flanks, two neutral wingers play against one defender.
- The neutral winger plays for the team in possession, which must try to score via an attack down the flank.
- If the defenders win the ball, the game starts again from the center line or on the other flank zone.

Variations
- Play 2 against 2 on the flanks.

**OBJECTIVE:**
- Improving passing technique.
- Improving the first and second touch when receiving a pass.

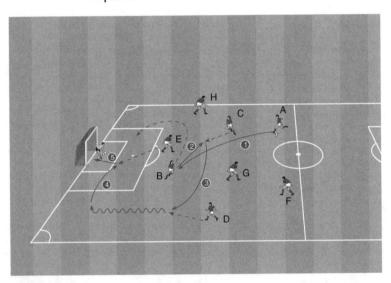

**ORGANIZATION:**
- Two teams of 8 players consisting of:
  two defenders,
  two defensive midfielders,
  one attacking midfielder,
  two wingers and one striker.

**INSTRUCTIONS:**
- 8 players (A-H) are positioned in one half of a full sized pitch, in front of a goal defended by a goal-keeper.
- Player A plays a high diagonal ball to player B, who passes to player C, who is making a forward run.
- Player C hits a long pass through the air or along the ground to player D, who is making a forward run down the left wing.
- Player D runs with the ball to the end line and crosses to B and E, who are running in at the goal.
- Players B and E try to score.
- Player F starts the game again with a high pass to player E, who lays the ball back to player G, who is making a forward run, and player G passes to player H on the wing.

**OBJECTIVE:** Improving combination play in midfield and making a forward run to support a striker.

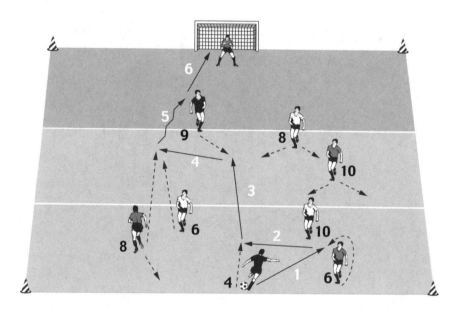

**ORGANIZATION:**

- Game of 3v3 with two neutral players.
- The game is played in two zones.
- Players are not obliged to stay in one zone.
- Ensure that two players stay close to the ball and one plays in a forward position.
- When you have possession, play 3v2 in one zone, trying to play the ball forward (striker or central midfielder).
- When the ball is played forward, one player from each team moves forward too.
- Play 3v2 again. After a 1-2 combination with the striker (neutral player), you can run with the ball toward the goal.
- When the defenders win the ball, they play a 1-2 combination with the neutral player and become the attackers.

- Make sure the players are positioned properly (2 players near the ball, 1 forward).
- Play the ball forward as quickly as possible.
- If it is not possible to play the ball forward, try to keep possession.
- Move in opposite directions (communicate with each other); central midfielder comes to the ball, left or right midfielder makes a forward run.
- Move in opposite directions relative to the neutral players (create space).
- Play the ball in firmly.

**OBJECTIVE:**  Improving defensive play.

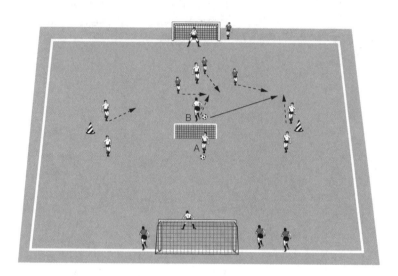

**ORGANIZATION:**
- 4 attackers against 3 defenders.
- The focus is on pushing towards the wing where the ball is.
- The aim is to screen the goal.
- You can change round after each goal, or play a competitive game.
- Success: attackers have to score 5 goals, defenders 4!

**INSTRUCTIONS:**
- Watch the ball.
- Push toward the ball.

**OBJECTIVE:**   Improving defensive play.

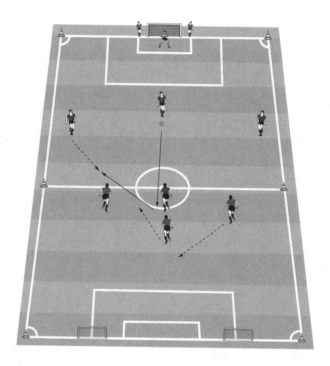

**ORGANIZATION:**
- The 4 attackers can score in the 2 small goals when they are in the opposition's half.
- The 3 defenders can play the ball to one of the two neutral players in the opposition's half and then score in the large goal.

**INSTRUCTIONS:**

Defenders individually
- Don't let your opponent get past you.
- Be focused in 1v1 situations.
- Don't make any mistakes!
- Stay on your feet, otherwise you are out of the play.

Defenders collectively
- Watch the ball and your opponent.
- Push toward the wing where the ball is.
- Communicate with your teammates.

Improving positional play and getting forward.

**ORGANIZATION:** Rectangle measuring 12x24 yards, divided into two equal zones.

**INSTRUCTIONS:**
- Positional game of 4v2 + 1 (v1).
- Play 4v2, keeping possession, and if possible pass to the forward player in the other zone.
- The forward player must lay the first pass off.
- His teammates must get forward as fast as possible to support him and play to keep possession again.
- One of the four players stays back and becomes the new forward player.
- If the players carry out the move successfully, the team scores a point.
- The defenders defend for an agreed number of minutes.

**OBJECTIVE:**
- Learning to play a forward pass.
- Learning to pass the ball forward with the first touch.

**ORGANIZATION:**
- Four players attack a small goal and 2 of the other four players are defenders.
- The other 2 players wait behind their own goal.
- After the attackers either try to score or lose the ball, 2 of the attackers become defenders and the other 2 players go behind their own goal.
- The other four players become the attackers.
- Practice or competitive game (which group of 2 sees a chance to score against its four opponents?).

Attackers:
- Use the foot furthest away from the passer to receive the ball (stand diagonally to the direction of the pass).
- Attackers can only touch the ball twice.
- Pass the ball forward if possible, preferably with the first touch.
- Move the ball square more quickly in order to be able to be finally able to pass it forward.

Defenders:
- Prevent the ball from being passed forward.
- Fake a challenge for the ball and try to block any gaps through which the ball might be played forward.
- Cover each other's backs.

**OBJECTIVE:** Improving build-up play.

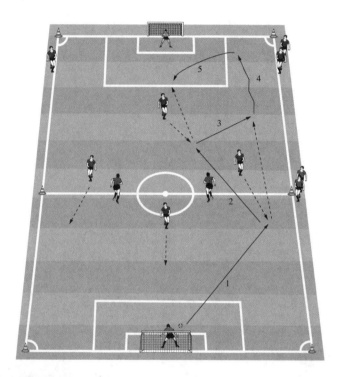

**ORGANIZATION:**
- The goalkeeper starts by playing the ball to one of the defenders.
- The advanced striker must always lay off the first ball to the player making the forward run.
- Then play 4 + goalkeeper against 2 + goalkeeper.

**INSTRUCTIONS:**

Defenders
- Make sure you are in space so that the ball can be played to you.
- Stand diagonally to the direction of the pass.
- If you are not in space, try again.

Keeper
- Try to play the ball to the defenders so that it is easy to control.
- Communicate with the defenders.

| **OBJECTIVE:** | Improving positional play when in possession. |

| **ORGANIZATION:** | - One team of 4 players and one of 3 players and a goalkeeper.<br>- Narrow playing area in one half of the pitch.<br>- Two cones mark an imaginary line at a distance of 3/4 of the length of the pitch from the end line. |

| **INSTRUCTIONS:** | - Build-up play starts at the goalkeeper.<br>- The attackers fall back until they are close to the imaginary line between the cones.<br>- The team building up the attack can score in the empty goal after passing the imaginary line.<br>- Coach continuously during the play. |

**OBJECTIVE:**
- After losing possession, immediately put pressure on the ball and try to regain possession.
- Don't be afraid to play the ball to the goalkeeper.
- Don't hide, don't play long balls.

**ORGANIZATION:**
- A playing area measuring 15 by 20 yards.
- The team in possession and the goalkeeper try to score in one of the two small goals.

**INSTRUCTIONS:**
Touch the ball twice (including ball contact by the goalkeeper).

**OBJECTIVE:**
- Careful build-up from the back.
- Strikers move into position to receive a pass at the right moment (read the play).

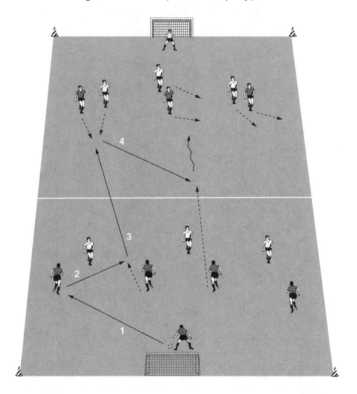

**ORGANIZATION:**
- A playing area measuring 30 by 25 yards.
- The size of the playing area depends on the level of skill of the players.
- Create scoring chances in a game of 4v4 including goalkeeper.

**INSTRUCTIONS:**
- Number of ball contacts.
- Play the ball straight to the goalkeeper.
- Strikers must lay the ball off to one of the central defenders who has not played the ball in.
- A goal has to be scored within 20 seconds.
- The game always starts with the defending team.

**OBJECTIVE:**  Improving build-up down the flanks.

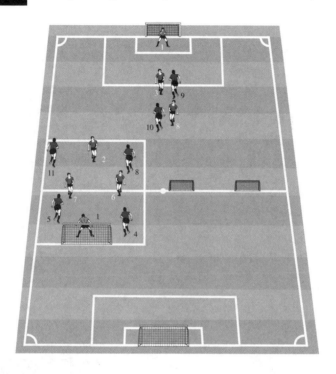

**ORGANIZATION:**  In a marked zone, 1 goalkeeper and 4 players play against 3 defenders.

**INSTRUCTIONS:**  Depending on the level of the players:
- Free play.
- Free play for group of 3/limited number of contacts by goalkeeper and group of 4.

Tasks of group of three:
- Win the ball.
- Try to score in the goal.

Tasks of goalkeeper and group of four:
- Keep the ball.
- Try to play the ball to the free man.
- Wait for the right moment to start an attack and break out.

**OBJECTIVE:**   Improving attacking play.

**ORGANIZATION:**

- 3v1 in the build-up zone and 4v3 + goalkeeper in the attacking zone.
- The group of three in the build-up zone is under pressure from the defenders and tries to play the ball to the attackers.
- After the pass, 4 play against 3 + goalkeeper in the attacking zone.
- Attackers score in the large goal.
- Defenders score by playing the ball to the defender in other zone.

Switch: After 5 attempts, the attackers swap places with the build-up players and the defender in the build-up zone is replaced by another defender.

Advanced striker
- Ensure that you are always available to receive a pass.
- Check away and check back to create space to receive a pass.
- If you are not in space, try again.

Player who passes into the attacking zone
- Play the ball away from the defender.
- Pay attention to the speed of the ball.
- Play the pass to your teammate in such away that he can easily control it.

Improving the use of the switch pass.

**ORGANIZATION:**
- 4v3 (with goalkeeper).
- Half of a full sized pitch.
- The game is always started in the center circle by the central midfielder.

**INSTRUCTIONS:**
- The attackers try to exploit their numerical advantage by means of a switch pass.
- The defenders have to mark their opponents closely on the flank where the ball is. As a result, the winger on the other flank has more space.
- The attackers look for an opportunity to switch the play to the other flank.
- The attackers score in the goal defended by the goalkeeper.
- The defenders score in the junior goals.
- The offside rule applies.
- No throw-ins or goal kicks. The game always starts at the central midfielder.

**OBJECTIVE:** Creating a scoring chance and preventing a fast counterattack.

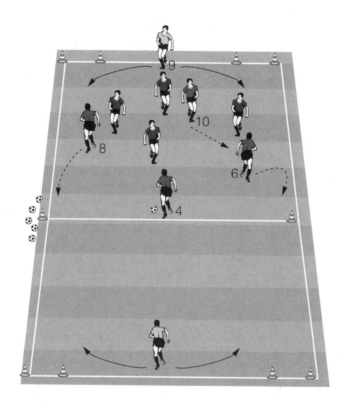

**ORGANIZATION:**
- Two zones with an additional player at each end line.
- Team A always starts with the ball in the opposition's half.
- Team A tries to find or create space for a decisive pass.
- Team A can score by dribbling the ball through the end zones on the end line.
- If team A loses possession, there is a lot of space behind it in which the opposition can score (also two end zones).

**INSTRUCTIONS:**

When in possession
- Pass forward rather than square.
- Pass square rather than back; wait for the right moment.
- Check away and back again to wrongfoot the defender.

When possession is lost
- Close off the center.
- Close up.
- Mark closely when danger threatens.

# SMALL SIDED GAMES (4v4) **113**

**OBJECTIVE:** Improving cooperation between strikers, midfielders and defenders in order to exert pressure on the ball in the opposition's half and disturb the opposing team's build-up play as early as possible.

**ORGANIZATION:**
- Playing area measuring 25 x 15 yards.
- Sufficient balls in the goals.
- Small sided game of 4 against 4 with 2 goalkeepers.
- The game is always started by the goalkeeper.

**INSTRUCTIONS:**
- When in possession: Try to build-up an attack and score.
- When the opposition has the ball: Pressure the ball and disturb the build-up play.

Technique when the opposition has the ball:
- Knees slightly bent.
- One foot in front of the other, ready to sprint.
- Fake a challenge for the ball.

Tactics when the opposition has the ball:
- Work together to pressure the opposition.
- Last man communicates with the others.
- Prevent the opposition from playing a forward pass.

# SMALL SIDED GAMES (4v4)

**OBJECTIVE:**
- Improving the response to losing possession.
- Improving the response to gaining possession.

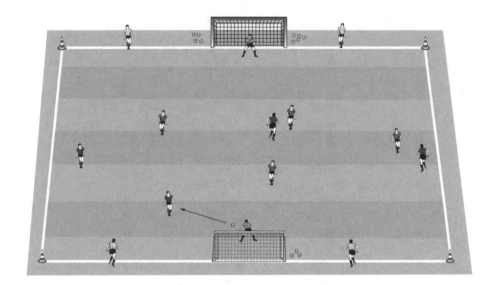

**ORGANIZATION:**
- Playing area measuring 30x30 yards.
- Two large goals.
- Three sets of colored vests.
- Small cones to mark out the playing area.
- Sufficient balls around the field.

**INSTRUCTIONS:**
Tactics
Choice
- "Make the right choice between getting the ball forward quickly or getting the ball into space and slowing the play down. If the opposition is disorganized, you should try to score as quickly as possible."
Make a run
- "After passing, run into space so you are available to receive the ball. Make fake runs and sudden accelerations off the ball."

Practicing cutting the ball.

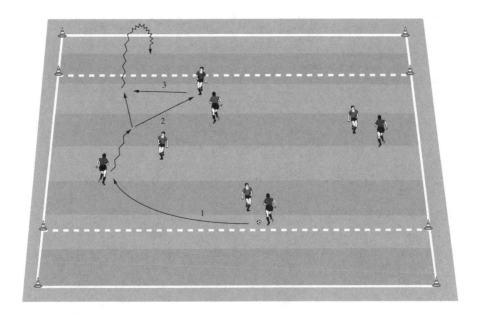

**ORGANIZATION:**
- Four against four. A player scores by dribbling the ball over the opposition's end line, cutting the ball behind his standing foot and then controlling the ball in the end zone.
- The players must have enough time to make the movement, otherwise they will be challenged by a defender, as the defenders can also enter the end zone.

**INSTRUCTIONS:**
- Variations: 1v1, 2v2, 3v3.
- Wider or longer playing area.

**OBJECTIVE:**   Improving ball-oriented defensive play.

**ORGANIZATION:**
- Game of 4v4.
- Two teams of four players.

**INSTRUCTIONS:**
- The blue team tries to dribble through one of the three zones.
- After winning possession, the red team tries to dribble through the zone marked by two cones (width about 20 yards).
- The offside rule applies.

**OBJECTIVE:**  Improving ball-oriented defensive play.

**ORGANIZATION:**
- Game of 4v4 with one large goal defended by a goalkeeper.
- Two teams of four players.

**INSTRUCTIONS:**
- Player F plays the ball in from behind the marked line and then joins in the game.
- If the defenders intercept the ball, they can score by dribbling the ball over the marked line.
- The offside rule applies.

**OBJECTIVE:** Improving ball-oriented defensive play.

**ORGANIZATION:**
- Game of 4v4 with one large goal defended by a goalkeeper.
- Two teams of four players.

**INSTRUCTIONS:**
- The last player of the blue team starts the attack.
- If the defenders intercept the ball, they can score by dribbling the ball over one of the two marked lines.
- The offside rule applies.

**OBJECTIVE:** Improving the response to a change of possession.

**ORGANIZATION:**
- Three teams of four players with two goalkeepers.
- One team fulfils the role of lay-off players on the end line for the attacking team.

**INSTRUCTIONS:**
- Build up speed of action.
- Improve sharpness and timing of run into space to receive the ball in front of goal and score.
- Improving the response to winning possession. Play the ball forward to the lay-off players near the goal and get forward quickly to support them.
- Improving the response to losing possession. In view of the small number of players, limited space and large goals, preventing scoring attempts is essential.
- Improving scoring from crosses (lay-off players on the side lines; 2-touch play).

**OBJECTIVE:**
- Improving speed of play when in possession, under pressure from the opposition.
- Improving the level of enjoyment of the players.

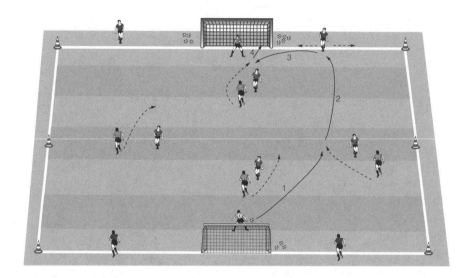

**ORGANIZATION:**
- Playing area measuring 30 by 20 yards.
- Two large goals.
- Playing area is marked out by cones.
- Sufficient balls around the playing area and in both goals.

**INSTRUCTIONS:**
- Game of 4v4 with four lay-off players and two goalkeepers.
- Score after a lay-off.
- No corners.
- Kick-in instead of throw-in.
- A goal cannot be scored directly from a kick-in.
- Neutral players are replaced every 3 minutes, goalkeepers remain.

**OBJECTIVE:**
- Learning when to play the ball forward and when to concentrate on keeping possession.
- Learning how to time a forward run to support the strikers.

**ORGANIZATION:**
- Two large goals with sufficient balls in each.
- Half of a full sized pitch.
- Fourteen players, including four lay-off players and two goalkeepers.
- Playing area measuring about 30 x 25 yards, marked out by cones, in the middle of the pitch.

**INSTRUCTIONS:**
Technique
Pass
- 'Play a firm pass to the advanced players. Trust that the players have the technique to control the ball.'
Finishing
- 'Concentrate on your shooting technique! Don't just try to hit the ball as hard as you can but try to place it.'

Tactics
Running onto the ball
- 'Don't stand too close to the lay-off players when your team has possession. You have to run onto the ball when it is laid off.'

**OBJECTIVE:**    Rapid ball circulation.

**ORGANIZATION:**
- Free play.
- The neutral players on the flanks can touch the ball twice, and the ones on the end line once.
- The offside rule applies.

**INSTRUCTIONS:**
- Use the width and length of the playing area.
- If your team loses possession, switch to zonal defending.

# SMALL SIDED GAMES 123
## (4v4+3)+K

**OBJECTIVE:**

- Recognizing when to play the ball forward to the striker.
- Improving the response to a change of possession.

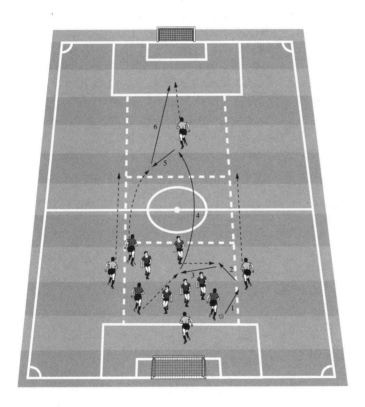

**ORGANIZATION:**

- Play down the center of the field.
- Divide the field into two equal zones and a smaller neutral middle zone.
- This middle zone ensures that the ball has to be played over a longer distance.
- The size of the two equal zones depends on the number of players.
- For 4v4 in one zone, 20 x 20 yards per zone is a good size, but take account of the level of skill of the players.

Rapid ball circulation
- 'Pass the ball at pace. Keep the ball circulating quickly.'

Run line
- 'Keep moving, always try to be available to receive a pass, and don't stand in front of the "lay-off player" player. Don't stand in a straight line with your teammates. Make sure that one defender can't cut out two of the players of the team in possession.'

Contact
- 'Stay in contact with the advanced striker and look for an opportunity to play the ball forward. If you play the ball forward, look to see whether a teammate can get forward to receive the lay-off.'

Getting forward in support
- 'Fake a run to wrongfoot your opponent. Watch where your teammates are.'

**OBJECTIVE:**
- Learning how to run into space.
- Improving play when in possession.

**ORGANIZATION:**
- 40 by 20 yards.
- Four cones.
- Sufficient balls around the field.
- Three colored vests.
- Three neutral players (one on each flank and one in the middle).
- Series of about 4 to 5 minutes (signs of tiredness).
- 11 to 15 players.

**INSTRUCTIONS:**

Technique
Receiving the ball
- 'Try to control the ball with your first touch so that you can immediately pass or go. In this game you almost always have passing options so you can get into space again quickly.'

Tactics
Keep moving
- 'Make a run after a run. Always try to get into a better position.'
Think ahead
- 'Before the ball reaches you, you should know what you want to do with it.'

**OBJECTIVE:**  Improving build-up play down the middle.

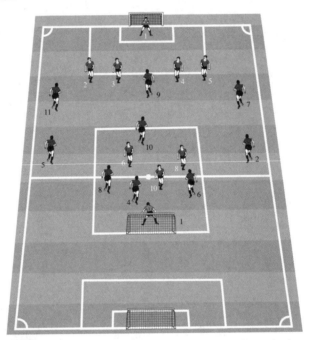

**ORGANIZATION:**  1 goalkeeper and 4 players play against 3 defenders in a marked out playing area.

**INSTRUCTIONS:**  Depending on the level of the players:
- Free play.
- Free play by group of three players/limited number of ball contacts by goalkeeper and group of four players.

Tasks of group of three:
- Win the ball.
- Try to score in the goal.

Tasks of goalkeeper and group of four:
- Keep the ball.
- Try to pass to the free player.
- Wait for the right moment to start an attack and break out.

**OBJECTIVE:**
- Learning how to win possession of the ball in your own half of the field when at a numerical disadvantage.
- Learning how to cover each other's backs.
- Learning how to play for offside.

**ORGANIZATION:**
- Half of a full sized pitch.
- One large goal and two small ones.
- Vests for both teams.
- Sufficient balls near the center spot.

**INSTRUCTIONS:**

Technique
Posture
- 'Defend with one foot diagonally in front of the other.'
Using your body.
- 'Use your body when an attacker starts a run.'
Shooting
- 'After winning the ball, shoot at one of the two small goals in order to score.'

Tactics
Communication
- 'Communicate with the players in front of you, because you have a better overview of the situation.'
Intercepting a forward pass
- 'The goalkeeper should not be frightened to stand as far as possible in front of his goal.
- Cover each other's backs.

Recognizing moments when you are faced with a choice.

**ORGANIZATION:**
- 5v4 + goalkeeper.
- Try to recognize moments when you have to choose what to do. Individuals must be able to make use of their own creativity and it is important that they make choices themselves. Discuss specific choices afterwards.

**INSTRUCTIONS:**
- Be ready to receive the ball, with your weight on the front of your feet, standing at an angle to the line of the pass.
- If the ball comes directly at your body, control the ball so that you can play it in the direction you want to.
- If the ball comes behind you, take a step back to receive the ball and then make a run toward the end line.
- Choose which cross to make (high, low, firm, looping).
- You don't always have to go all the way to the end line to be able to play a good cross.

Learning what options are available for build-up play from a goal kick when the opposing team plays with three strikers.

- One fixed goal.
- Two junior goals.
- Width of penalty area plus ten yards left or right, and 55 yards long.
- At least ten players.

Technique
Passing (goalkeeper)
- 'Play the ball hard and cleanly in the direction of your teammate. This gains you speed and time.'
Receiving the ball (all build-up players)
- 'Control the ball with your fist touch so that you can go or pass with the second touch. Listen to what your teammates tell you.'

Tactics

Call for the ball (central defenders)

- 'Don't be frightened to take the initiative and call for the ball.

Playing a forward pass (all build-up players)

- 'The ultimate aim of the build-up is to score a goal. So pass the ball forward when you can!'

Communication (all build-up players)

- 'Communicate with your teammates. Should a teammate play a first-time pass or turn with the ball? Tell him what to do.'

**OBJECTIVE:**   Learning to get the ball forward.

**ORGANIZATION:**
- At each end of the field is a zone 10 yards deep.
- In front of the zone is the offside line.

**INSTRUCTIONS:**
- You can score by passing to a teammate who controls the ball in the zone.
- The defenders are not allowed to enter the zone.
- When the pass is made, the defenders can intercept the ball in the zone.
- Before making a forward run:
- Fake a run toward the ball and then check back and make a forward run.
- Get behind the defender and make a diagonal run from behind his back.
- Go wide and make a run down the flank.

**OBJECTIVE:** Strikers run into space when their defenders have the ball.

**ORGANIZATION:**
- Three zones.
- No one can enter the middle zone.

**INSTRUCTIONS:**
- In zone 1, four defenders and a holding midfielder play against four midfielders.
- In zone 3, three strikers play against four defenders.
- In zone 1, the five players try to exploit their numerical advantage to create the space needed to make a forward pass to their strikers.

# SMALL SIDED GAMES (5v5)

**OBJECTIVE:**  Responding quickly to a change of possession.

**ORGANIZATION:**
- Two groups of five players.
- A playing area measuring 50 by 30 yards.

**INSTRUCTIONS:**
- Each team has two players on the end line of the opposing team.
- The players are numbered from 1 to 7. When the game starts, numbers 1 and 2 are on the end line of the zone in which their team can score.
- The players switch positions every two minutes.
- Numbers 3 and 4, 5 and 6, 7 and 1, 2 and 3, 4 and 5, and 6 and 7 go in turn, at 2 minute intervals, to the end line of the zone in which their team can score.
- They themselves cannot score.
- When possession changes, the teams must respond immediately.
- The playing area is relatively small, so the team that wins possession can score relatively quickly.

**OBJECTIVE:**    Improving technical skills.

**ORGANIZATION:**
- Half of a full sized pitch with a strip three yards wide along each side line.
- Sufficient balls beside both goals.

**INSTRUCTIONS:**

Technique
Receiving (players on the side lines).
- 'Receive and go. In this game you can often cross the ball from the flank. Get the ball into position to cross as soon as you can.
Passing
- 'Play firm passes. Short passes with the inside of the foot. Longer passes with the instep. Keep the ball low by getting your body over the ball as you pass it.'

Tactics
Triangles
- 'There are lots of triangles on the field. Try to make use of them.'
In front of the receiver
- 'Play the ball into the path of the receiver, so that he doesn't have to wait for it and the ball circulates quickly.'

**OBJECTIVE:**
- Encourage flank play.
- Improving crossing and run lines.

**ORGANIZATION:**
- The 2 wingers can only play in the attacking zone (opposition's half).
- The 2 wingers must start from the flank zone.

**INSTRUCTIONS:**
- Create a numerical advantage.
- Respond to change of possession.

**OBJECTIVE:** Improving attacking play

**ORGANIZATION:**
- The ball is played in by the coach.
- The two neutral players are restricted to 2 ball contacts when they receive the ball.
- The attackers try to score and the defenders try to dribble the ball over the dotted line.
- The wingers must call for the ball and form a threat to the opposition.
- Finish with a small sided game (7v7 with 2 large goals defended by goalkeepers).

**INSTRUCTIONS:** The strikers must make runs to get into space and receive the ball. When the team loses possession, they must fall back into the middle of the pitch and cover the opposing players.

Practicing getting into the operational zones to surprise the opposition, create chances and score goals.

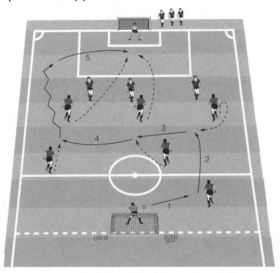

**ORGANIZATION:**
- Use three quarters of a full sized pitch.
- The two defending trios switch after five games.

**INSTRUCTIONS:**
- The goalkeeper throws the ball to the right back.
- The right midfielder moves a short distance inside.
- The outside right falls back.
- The outside right indicates where he wants the ball.
- The right back passes to the winger.
- The outside right passes first time to the right half, who moves toward the center of the field.
- When the outside right passes, the striker makes a run into the space left by the outside right, and the outside left makes a run into the space left by the striker.
- This creates space for the left midfielder to make a forward run and cross the ball.
- The three strikers must take up good positions in front of the goal (near post, a short distance behind the near post and on the edge of the penalty area) and try to score.
- The three defenders only have to win the ball in the air to score.

**OBJECTIVE:** Improving the timing and execution of passes from the deepest midfielders to the strikers. Cooperation between strikers and the advanced midfielders, with the continuation of the move and the play in front of the goal.

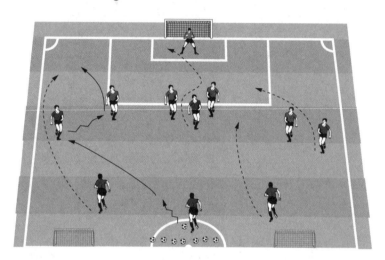

**ORGANIZATION:**
- 6v4 (and one goalkeeper).
- Half of a full sized pitch.
- Two small goals.

**INSTRUCTIONS:**
- The six players try to score in the large goal defended by the goalkeeper.
- The four players and the goalkeeper defend and try to score in the small goals on the center line.
- When the ball is kicked in or a goal kick is taken, the game starts again with the central midfielder.
- When the players have become accustomed to the routine, the backs play at 100% rather than 75%. Because the midfielder can also dribble the ball in or play in the central striker, the backs have to leave the wingers a certain amount of space. The objective is therefore to play the first ball deep, after which the players must make their runs.

# SMALL SIDED GAMES (6v4) 137

**OBJECTIVE:**

- Improving attacking play down the flanks
- Improving crossing skills

**ORGANIZATION:**

- Half of a full sized pitch.
- One large goal.
- Two small goals.
- Zones on the side lines for the wingers.
- Vests for both teams.
- Sufficient balls near the center line.

**INSTRUCTIONS:**

Technique
- First-time pass
- 'First-time passing is important for a winger. Play the ball back so that the receiver can easily play the ball forward for you to run on to, i.e. you pass and go.'

Receive and go
- 'Run with the ball toward the end line.'

Run with the ball
- 'Run with the ball at top speed. If you have a lot of space, you can push the ball further away from your foot.'

Cross
- 'Get behind the ball before you cross. If you do this, the cross is no more difficult than passing a rolling ball.'

# SMALL SIDED GAMES (6v5) **138**

**OBJECTIVE:** Improving the cooperation between the goalkeeper and the defenders during build-up play.

**ORGANIZATION:**
- Half of a full sized pitch.
- The six players try, together with the goalkeeper, to build up a good attack and score by dribbling the ball over the center line.
- The five players try to prevent this and score in the large goal.

**INSTRUCTIONS:**
- Play the ball in firmly to the correct foot (you must know which foot is the goalkeeper's strongest).
- Stand at an angle to the path of the ball so that you can quickly receive it and go.
- Decide whether it is the right moment to move into space to receive a pass or whether you should stay where you are.
- Communicate to make things easier for each other.

**OBJECTIVE:** Improving build-up play.

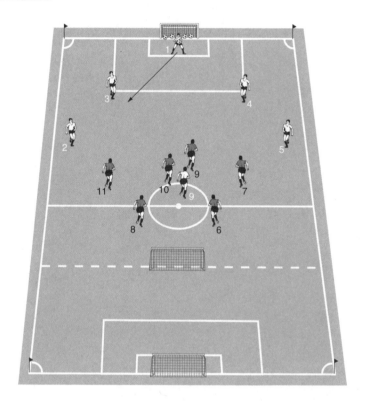

**ORGANIZATION:**
- A team of 6 players and a team of 5 players and a goalkeeper.
- Lots of balls near the goalkeeper.
- The empty goal is 70 yards from the end line.

**INSTRUCTIONS:**
- The build up always starts at the goalkeeper.
- The attackers fall back to the front of the center circle.
- The attacking team can score in the empty goal beyond the center line.
- Coach as the situation requires it.

# SMALL SIDED GAMES (6v6)+2N **140**

**OBJECTIVE:**
- Improving passing to the central strikers.
- Improving the forward runs of the midfielders after the pass to the strikers.

**ORGANIZATION:**
- Playing area measuring 25 by 40 yards.
- In the orientation phase, keep things simple.

**INSTRUCTIONS:**
- Balance between players who call for the ball and players who stay away from the ball.
- Focus on technical and tactical execution.

**OBJECTIVE:** Improving combination play.

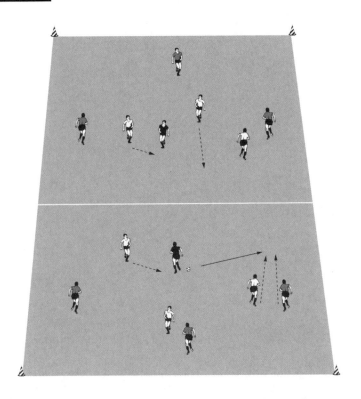

**ORGANIZATION:** The two neutral players are always in the center and always play for the team in possession.

**INSTRUCTIONS:**
- Encourage combination play when in possession. Always look for a short passing option before playing the ball into space.
- Encourage the defenders to close down the available space and the passing and long ball options.
- Encourage communication and fast switching of the ball to the other flank.

**OBJECTIVE:**
- Preventing a quick counter attack.
- Improving the response to a change of possession.

**ORGANIZATION:**
- Two teams of 6 players, each with 1 neutral player.
- 6v6 in one half of the field, with one neutral player.

**INSTRUCTIONS:**
The team without the ball tries to win possession and then play the ball to the neutral player in the other half.

**OBJECTIVE:**
- Improving cooperation between midfielders and strikers.
- Choosing the right moment to make a diagonal pass.

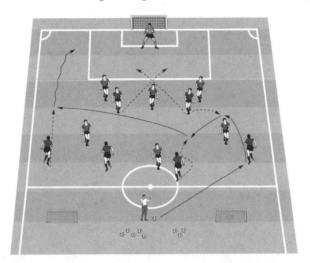

**ORGANIZATION:**
- Half of a full sized pitch plus 15 yards.
- One team plays in a 4:2 formation.
- The other team (plus a goalkeeper) plays in a 1:3:2:1 formation.
- The coach plays the ball in from the middle of the end line behind the midfielders.
- There are two small goals in which the defenders can score.
- Each player remains in his fixed position as much as possible.

**INSTRUCTIONS:**
- The coach starts the game by playing the ball to a midfielder.
- The midfielder tries to pass to a striker.
- A central midfielder makes a forward run and the striker lays the ball off to him.
- A midfielder makes a forward run along the flank and the central midfielder makes a diagonal pass him.
- The midfielder crosses to the two strikers, whose runs cross as they close in on goal.
- The attacking team tries to score in the large goal defended by a goalkeeper.
- The defending team tries to score in the two small goals.

**OBJECTIVE:** Improving positional play in the final third of the field.

**ORGANIZATION:**
- Team A plays in a 1:2:3:1 formation.
- Team A's goalkeeper plays the ball to 6, 8 or 10 to start the game.
- Team A has to score twice within 8 minutes to win, otherwise team B wins.
- Team B (1:4:1:1) wins if it scores one goal.
- If the ball goes out of play, the game resumes with team A in possession.
- Initially team B is well organized and team A finds scoring difficult. Team A must react quickly if it loses possession, as team B only needs to score one goal to win. If team A win the ball back, team B will probably not be so well organized, so there will be more space for team A.

**INSTRUCTIONS:**
Team that is not in possession
- Communicate about who should pressure the ball, and where.
- Cover each other's backs.
- Make sure the opposition cannot play a long ball forward.

**OBJECTIVE:** Improving wing play.

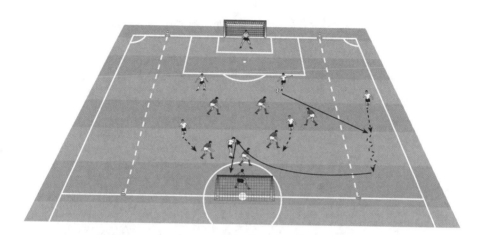

**ORGANIZATION:**
- Three teams of 6 players (in specific positions).
- Half of a full sized pitch with 2 large goals and marked zones along each side (neutral zones).

**INSTRUCTIONS:**
- 6v6 with 2 goalkeepers.
- After 10 passes, the ball must be played down the flanks; only attackers can enter the neutral zone and cross the ball.
- Three games of 8 minutes each (everyone against everyone).

**OBJECTIVE:** Improving build-up play.

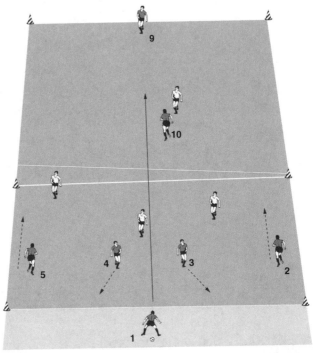

**ORGANIZATION:**
- Scoring by defenders: from the goalkeeper's position, playing the ball directly or indirectly to the other flank without losing possession wins one point.
- Scoring by attackers: from the position of one lay-off player, playing the ball directly or indirectly to the other lay-off player wins one point.
- The zone in which the positional play takes place is important; select a zone 20 to 25 yards wide from the inside the penalty area to the center line.

**INSTRUCTIONS:**
- Lay-off players stand at an angle to the path of the ball and subsequently move further up the pitch.
- Players 3 and 4 stand at an angle to the path of the ball and take up positions where the player with the ball can pass to them.

**OBJECTIVE:**  Improving cooperation between attackers and midfielders when the attackers are in possession in the opposition's half.

**ORGANIZATION:**  -Full width of the field and 65 yards long.
-Two small goals and one large goal.
-Both teams wear vests.

**INSTRUCTIONS:**  Tactics
Calling for the ball at the right moment (strikers).
- 'Call for the ball when you have contact with the player in possession if he is in a position to pass and you are in a better position than him.'
Pass the ball at the right moment (midfielders).
- 'Pay attention to when the strikers run into position for a pass. They might check away and then check back again for a pass, or they might call for the ball or point to where they want the ball.'
Check away and back again at the right moment (strikers).
'Make a run if you have the space, or if a teammate tells you to. Always be on the lookout for chances of getting forward.'
Communication
- 'Communicate with each other. Help each other by being clear and confident!'

- Learning how to quickly play a forward pass to a midfielder or a striker during the build-up play.
- Learning how to support a midfielder or striker after a forward pass.

**ORGANIZATION:**
- Half of a full sized pitch.
- One large goal and two small goals.
- Sufficient balls beside the large goal.
- Vests for both teams.

**INSTRUCTIONS:**
Tactics
Wait
- 'Wait for the right moment to play the ball forward. You have a numerical advantage so it should always be possible to find an unmarked player.'
Play the ball quickly
- 'If you can play the ball quickly, then you should do so. This gives the opposition less time to reorganize.'
Linking up
- 'If we play the ball forward, the opposition will pressure the player in possession. Teammates must get forward so that he can lay the ball off to them.'

# SMALL SIDED GAMES (7v6) **149**

**OBJECTIVE:**
- Pressing the ball.
- When in possession, playing the ball into space immediately with a long pass.
- Switching the play when the opposition exerts pressure.

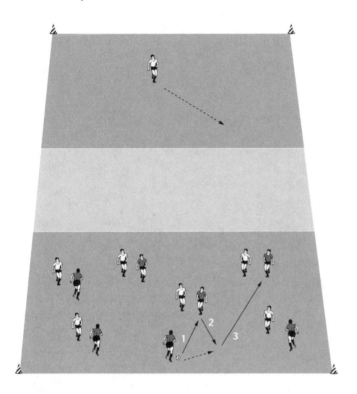

**ORGANIZATION:**
- The size of the playing area depends on the level of skill of the players.
- If the team of six wins the ball, it tries to pass to the player in the other zone as quickly as possible.
- All players then cross into the other zone except one player from the green team.

**INSTRUCTIONS:**
- Number of touches of the ball.
- The player in the other zone who receives the pass must lay the ball off.

Improving positional play in midfield with the emphasis on the team formation and cooperation between the players.

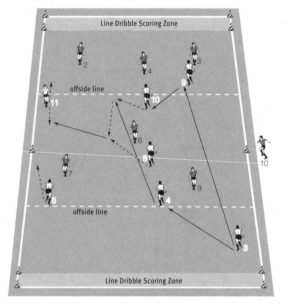

**ORGANIZATION:**
- The team in possession plays 7v6 with one man more.
- The team without the ball plays 6v7 with one man less.
- The positional game takes place in one half of the field.
- The left line plays against the right line.
- When a team wins possession, the advanced midfielder (10) of the opposing team drops out so that a 7v6 situation is created and the team in possession has one man more.
- When a team loses possession, its advanced midfielder (10) drops out and the team plays on with one man less.
- Teams score by means of a line dribble.

**INSTRUCTIONS:**
- Team formation.
- Player 4 comes toward the ball and player 5 creates space and moves further forward.
- Player 8 creates space for players 9 and 10 to move into, after which the ball can be laid off to player 8 or played directly to the winger.

**OBJECTIVE:**
- Improving positional play.
- Using the third man.

**ORGANIZATION:**
- Half of a full sized pitch.
- Four zones measuring 5 by 5 yards in the corners of the field.
- It must be possible to play all round the zones.
- Goals can be scored in the zones.

**INSTRUCTIONS:**

Technique
Passing
- 'Pass the ball firmly to keep the pace high.'
Receiving the ball
- 'When you receive the ball, make sure that you can immediately pass it or run with it.'
Lay-off
- The player who lays the ball off must be positioned so that he can play the ball to a third player. Look up and stand at an angle to the path of the ball.'

Tactics
- Coaching
- 'Coach the players as the ball circulates. Who is the pass intended for and what should he do? Should he lay it off or turn and go?'

**OBJECTIVE:**
- Improving awareness of the right moment to intervene in the opposition's build-up play.
- Improving awareness of opportunities to create scoring chances quickly when the ball is won.

**ORGANIZATION:**
- Half of a full sized pitch plus penalty area (three zones).
- Two goals.
- 14 players and 2 goalkeepers.

**INSTRUCTIONS:**
Tactics
Lines close together
- 'Do not let the lines get too far apart.'
Concentration
- 'Follow the opposition's build-up play. Be patient.'
Coaching
- 'Make sure that the players keep to their positions.'
Choosing the right moment to exert pressure
- 'Pressure the opposition when the ball is played in on the wing. Pressure the opposition players immediately.'
Change of possession
- 'When we win the ball we must try to get forward.'

- Learning how to defend against the opposition's build-up play.
- Learning how to win the ball during the opposition's build-up play.

**ORGANIZATION:**
- Small sided game of 8v7 (7v7 plus one goalkeeper).
- Formation 1:3:2:2 and 3:2:2.
- Three-quarters of a full sized pitch.
- One large goal with a goalkeeper, one large goal without a goalkeeper.

Technique
Knees
- 'Keep your knees bent slightly. This enables you to react and move faster.'
Ankles rigid
- 'You need to keep your ankles rigid when you make a sliding tackle or a block tackle.

Tactics
Prevent the opposition from playing the ball forward
- 'We want to prevent the opposition from playing the ball forward into the danger areas. We have to try to force them to play the ball square.'

Teamwork
-' Work together with the players who are closest to you. You cannot win the ball on your own. There is no point in trying to pressure the opposition players on your own.'

**OBJECTIVE:**
- Learning when to pass to the striker.
- Learning how to get forward to support the striker when the ball is played to him.

**ORGANIZATION:**
- Play up and down the field.
- Use slightly more than one half of length of the field.
- Use slightly less than the whole width of the field.
- The free zones measure about 40x15 yards.
- On the end line of the free zones are two small goals.

**INSTRUCTIONS:**
- Two permanent strikers in a free zone.
- Initially, no other players are allowed to enter the free zones.
- The play is started by a player on the edge of the free zone with the ball.
- By means of positional play, the players try to pass the ball to their striker in the free zone.
- When a pass is played to the striker, his teammates (midfielders) must try to get forward to support him and try to score.
- The defending team must try to prevent the opposition from scoring and also enter the free zone to achieve this.
- If a goal is scored directly from a lay-off by the striker (one touch play), the score counts double.

- Learning how to keep possession.
- Learning what to do when the team loses possession.
- Learning how to play to avoid conceding a goal.

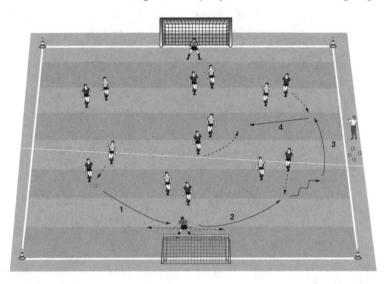

**ORGANIZATION:**
- 7v7 with two neutral players.
- The field is twice the size of the penalty area.
- Two large goals.
- Both goalkeepers join in the play in front of the goal.
- Use 5 balls; this is also the number of attempts that the team without the ball has to win the ball and score.
- As far as possible, the players stay in their own positions.

**INSTRUCTIONS:**
- The 7 players and the goalkeeper try to retain possession, as though they are in the lead and want to preserve it.
- They score a point if they keep possession for one minute.
- If they lose the ball, they try to regain possession.
- The team without the ball tries to gain possession and score in one of the two goals.
- The team without the ball has five attempts to win it.
- The ball is "out" after a scoring attempt, a goal or a change of possession.

- Improving cooperation between the four defenders against two strikers and one central midfielder, so that the ball is won more often.
- Learning what to do when the ball is won; don't pass forward blindly but play to keep possession.

- Half of a full sized field plus 20 yards over the center line.
- Sufficient balls around the field and in the goals for quick restarts.

- Small sided game of 7v7.
- The team being coached plays in a 1:3:3 formation.
- The team being coached has no striker, so the players do not have the option of trying to play a forward pass but must try to slow the play down by passing to the goalkeeper or the free central defender.
- The attacking team plays in a 4:2 formation.
- The attacking team has no goalkeeper and must try to play the ball to one of the strikers as quickly as possible.
- The defenders therefore have a lot of opportunities to close down the players in possession.
- The goalkeeper plays as far in front of his goal as possible so that he can remain in contact with his defenders.

**OBJECTIVE:** Learning how to pressure the opposing team it its own half after it wins possession.

**ORGANIZATION:**
- Use one half of a full sized pitch with two large goals.
- Sufficient balls beside both goals for fast restarts.
- Decide whether to coach one or both teams.

**INSTRUCTIONS:**
- Small sided game of 7v7 plus goalkeepers.
- Both teams play in a 1:3:1:3 formation.
- Let the players play as much as possible in their own positions.
- Emphasize that it is important to recognize the right moment to exert pressure:
  - when a throw-in is taken;
  - when a poor pass is made (not struck hard enough, or played through the air);
  - when a weaker opponent has the ball;
  - in the corners of the field.

**OBJECTIVE:**
- Exert pressure immediately after losing possession.
- Regain possession.
- Don't be afraid to pass to the goalkeeper.
- Don't hide, don't play long passes.

**ORGANIZATION:**
Playing area measuring 30 by 25 yards.

**INSTRUCTIONS:**
- The whites choose the right moment to exert pressure on the other team's build-up play.
- Specific coaching of the goalkeeper during the build-up.
- The greens exert pressure after losing possession.

**OBJECTIVE:** Improving cooperation between midfielders and strikers when the opposition is in possession.

**ORGANIZATION:**
- Play up and down the field.
- Field length 65 to 70 yards: half of a full sized field plus fifteen yards over the center line.
- Field width 50 to 60 yards: complete width of a full sized pitch or a little less.

**INSTRUCTIONS:**
Tactics
First move closer together
- 'When you lose possession or the opposition has possession, move closer together; the lines should be close together and the available space should be made smaller.'
Leave the flanks free
- 'We want the opposition to play down the wings so that we can exert pressure there.'

Communication
- 'Help each other by pressuring the opposition: central midfielders move to support the left and right midfielders.'
Rapid switch when possession is won
- 'When you win the ball, try to get forward quickly.'

**OBJECTIVE:** Improving cooperation between defenders and mid-fielders in breaking up and screening the opposing team's build-up in the defending team's half.

**ORGANIZATION:**
- Positional game of 7v8 with 2 goalkeepers.
- The game starts with the ball in the possession of the team of 8.
- The team of 7 must score within 1 minute.

**INSTRUCTIONS:**
- The team of 8 can initially score by dribbling the ball over the end line. Subsequently in the large goal.
- Formations 1:4:2:1 and 1:2:3:3. Other formations can be used.
- The offside rule applies.
- Adjust the space to suit the level of skill of the players.
- Read the opposing team's build-up play.
- Carry out basic tasks; maintain correct distance from each other, watch what your teammates are doing.
- Choose position.
- Communication (which side to screen?)
- Pressure the player in possession.
- Prevent a forward pass from being made.
- Force the team in possession to pass the ball square.
- Cover each other's back.

**OBJECTIVE:**
- Preventing a quick counter attack.
- Learning what to do when the team loses possession.

**ORGANIZATION:**
- A team of 7 players plays against a team of 8 players in one half of a full sized pitch.
- There are two small goals on the center line.

**INSTRUCTIONS:**
- The team being coached has one player less and tries to score in one of the two small goals when it has possession.
- Take no unnecessary risks.
- Chase/stay compact.
- Restart the game from the center line instead of taking corners.

**OBJECTIVE:**

Learning what to do when possession is regained; good, fast positional reaction, keep possession of the ball as long as possible.

**ORGANIZATION:**

- Rectangle measuring 20x40 yards, depending on players' age and level of skill.
- Twelve players.
- Divided into three teams (three times four).
- Or 15 players (three times five).

**INSTRUCTIONS:**

Technique
Receiving the ball
- 'The ball must be immediately ready to play after your first touch.'
Passing
- Pass the ball firmly. Don't lose time with slow passes.'

Tactics
Play the ball to the receiver's strongest foot
- 'When you pass, indicate which side you want the ball to be played to.'
Choice of long or short
- 'If there is space on the other flank, try to switch the play there via a second player.'
Take your time
- 'If you are not under pressure after winning possession, you can take your time and slow the play down.'

**OBJECTIVE:**
- Preventing a quick counter attack.
- Learning what to do when your team loses possession.

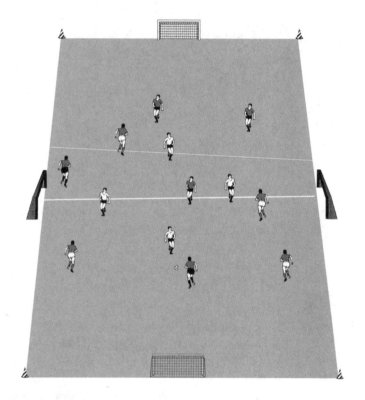

**ORGANIZATION:**     Three teams of 4 players.

**INSTRUCTIONS:**
- 8 players try to keep possession of the ball.
- The other 4 players try to win the ball and score in one of the four small goals.

**OBJECTIVE:**  Improving build-up play from the back.

**ORGANIZATION:**

- Playing field +/-10 yards over the center line so that the field can be divided into two halves, creating space for players to move up in support.
- The team of 8 plays in a 1:4:3 formation.
- The team of 5 plays in a 2:3 formation at first.

**INSTRUCTIONS:**

- Play the ball in firmly - "Your teammate has more time if you play the ball firmly. You make things easier for him."
- Laying the ball off - "By laying the ball off, you keep the speed of the ball circulation high. If possible, play the ball as quickly as possible. Get your body over the ball when you lay it off."
- Receiving the ball - "Control the ball with your first touch so that you can take it in the direction you want to go with the second touch."
- Get your body between the ball and your opponent - "Shield the ball if you cannot turn."
- Hold the ball - "Hold the ball at your feet if you have to wait for teammates to get forward and support you."

**OBJECTIVE:**
Improving build-up play, with the focus on passing the ball when under pressure from opponents, and what to do when there is a change of possession.

**ORGANIZATION:**
- 8v6.
- Playing area from the edge of one penalty area to the edge of the other, over the full width of the field.
- 1 large goal.
- Assistant coach plays the ball to the defenders from the side line. The defenders, under pressure from three attackers, must play the ball to their own attackers. The attackers, under pressure from 3 defenders, try to exploit their 4v3 advantage to score from outside the penalty area with a firm pass into the goal.

**INSTRUCTIONS:**
- If the 3 opposing attackers win the ball during the build-up play, they can score by dribbling the ball over the line.
- If the 3 defenders win the ball, they must play it to one of the two coaches on the side line.

**OBJECTIVE:**     Improving ball-oriented defending.

**ORGANIZATION:**     Small sided game of 8v6 with one large goal defended by a goalkeeper and three marked zones.

**INSTRUCTIONS:**
- The blue team (six players) tries to score in the large goal defended by a goalkeeper.
- The red team has eight players and tries to win the ball and then score by dribbling it through the cones on either the right or the left or passing it into the small goal between them.

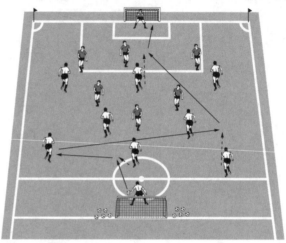

**OBJECTIVE:**
- Playing to retain possession by combining in close spaces.
- Switching the play from a crowded situation into space while under pressure from the opposition.

**ORGANIZATION:**
- Attackers in 3:2:3 formation.
- Defenders in 3:2:1 formation.
- 20 balls.
- Large portable goal.

**INSTRUCTIONS:**
Possession: build-up/attack
- Long forward pass to attackers at just the right moment.
- At the right moment, one of the strikers calls for the ball.
- Switch pass/crossfield pass.
- Team keeps good shape by means of positional play in close space.
- Players without the ball must take the initiative.
- Play long forward passes low and firmly; third player must take up position to receive lay-off.
- Stand at an angle to the path of the ball to receive it.

Defense
- The nearest player must exert pressure on the ball.
- Communication.
- Close down the space.
- Make sure you can see your direct opponent and the ball.

**OBJECTIVE:**
- Exert pressure immediately after losing the ball.
- Regain possession.
- Don't be afraid to play the ball to the goalkeeper.
- Don't hide, don't play long passes.

**ORGANIZATION:**
- Playing area measuring 30 by 25 yards.
- The team in green plays with both goalkeepers to keep possession.
- The team in white must try to score in either goal if it wins possession.
- The goalkeeper must not play the ball to the other goalkeeper.

**INSTRUCTIONS:**
Two-touch play.

**OBJECTIVE:** Improving ball-oriented defending.

**ORGANIZATION:** Small sided game of 8v7 with one large goal defended by a goalkeeper.

**INSTRUCTIONS:**
- The blue team (seven players) tries to score in the large goal defended by the goalkeeper.
- The red team has eight players and tries to win the ball and then score by dribbling over the line between the cones.

**OBJECTIVE:**
- Improving team tactics.
- Improving soccer-specific endurance.

**ORGANIZATION:**
- 2 teams play 8v8 with 4 neutral players.
- Use cones to mark a playing area between the penalty area and the center line.

**INSTRUCTIONS:**
-Lots of repetitions.
- The neutral players always play for the team in possession.
- Lots of repetitions.
- Allow sufficient rest periods between drills.
- The goalkeepers change places after each shot or after 2-3 shots.

Focus
- Man to man marking over the whole field; this improves soccer-specific endurance.

**OBJECTIVE:**
- Improving individual runs with the ball in a small sided game.
- Becoming familiar with the demands of demonstration coaching sessions.

**ORGANIZATION:**
- Field measuring 55x50 yards.
- Marked out with small cones.
- Sufficient balls near the end lines.

**INSTRUCTIONS:**
- 8v8 line soccer.
- Score by dribbling over the opposition's end line.
- Increase the emphasis on individual runs with the ball.

# SMALL SIDED GAMES (8v8)

**OBJECTIVE:**
- Getting the ball forward quickly.
- Fast attacking play.
- Increasing the speed of execution.

**ORGANIZATION:**
-16 players and 2 goalkeepers.
-3 zones.

**INSTRUCTIONS:**
- In zone A (defensive zone), no passing is allowed and the game always starts at the goalkeeper.
- In zone B (center zone), a maximum of three passes in sequence is allowed; the fourth pass must be into the attacking zone (C).
- In zone C (attacking zone), free play is allowed; the offside rule applies here.
- In zones A and B, 3-touch play is allowed.

Variations:
- Reduce the number of ball contacts.
- Only 2 passes are allowed in zone B.

**OBJECTIVE:**
- Free play is allowed in the center zone.
- Exploit the man against man situation.

**ORGANIZATION:**
- 16 players.
- 4 small goals.
- 4 zones.
- 1 center zone.

**INSTRUCTIONS:**
- A small sided game of 6v6 is played in the center zone.
- From the center zone, create a man against man situation with the player in zone A, B, C or D.
- 1 player is positioned in zones A, B, C and D.
- From the center zone, try to dribble to attacking zone A or B (C or D) and exploit the man against man situation.
- If possession of the ball is lost, the defender's position in the center zone is taken by another player.
- Free play; reduce number of ball contacts.

**OBJECTIVE:** Improving ball-oriented defense.

**ORGANIZATION:** Small sided game of 8v8 with two large goals defended by goalkeepers.

**INSTRUCTIONS:**
- One goal is 15 yards behind the center line.
- The offside rule applies.
- The defenders must communicate.
- Ensure that the lines are never too far apart.

**OBJECTIVE:** Developing soccer skills with the emphasis on ball circulation in a system of play where there is a one-man-more situation.

**ORGANIZATION:**
-8v8 (8:7+1).
-Length of field is 45 yards.
-Width of field is 25 yards.

**INSTRUCTIONS:**
- The team of 8 must try to keep possession while retaining its formation, and look for an opportunity to pass the ball forward.
- 8 defenders, 7 of them active (they try to win the ball) and the 8th with a free role.
- Note: Because the play is always in the same direction, each player retains his position (team functions), also when the opposition has the ball.

**OBJECTIVE:** Acquiring basic conditioning in a natural manner.

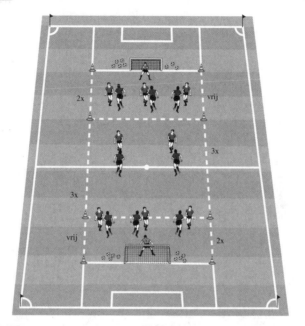

**ORGANIZATION:**
- Duration 4x8 minutes.
- Lots of space on the playing area.
- Technique and position are unimportant.
- The variations in free play and/or 1, 2 and 3-touch play are important for regulating the amount of work the players carry out.
- 3 ball contacts as a midfielder (lots of players around).
- 2 ball contacts in the defense (force players to run into space).
- Free play in the penalty area during an attack (more competitive).

**INSTRUCTIONS:**
- The players must do a lot of work.
- Dead moments such as throw-ins and corners must be avoided.
- The ball is brought into play quickly by the goalkeeper (lots of balls in the goal to ensure fast continuation of play).

**OBJECTIVE:** Learning how to work together with the three midfielders to put the three strikers under pressure when possession is lost, and thus to regain possession.

**ORGANIZATION:**
- 8v8 plus two goalkeepers.
- Three quarters of a full sized field.
- Balls in the goal of the goalkeeper who always starts the build-up play.
- Both teams wear vests.

Technique
Make yourself wide
- 'Make yourself as wide as possible with your knees bent and your weight on the front of the foot.'

Sliding tackle as a last resort
- 'Do not make a sliding tackle unless you are 100% certain that you can win the ball or have to commit a foul.'

Tactics
Correct timing
- 'Exert pressure when an opponent receives a difficult ball and your teammates behind you tell you to do so.'
- 'To be able to intercept the ball better, stand beside your opponent. If you stand behind him, he will block your path to the ball.'

**OBJECTIVE:** Improve your play after your team wins possession, by trying to pass the ball forward or switching the play to the other flank.

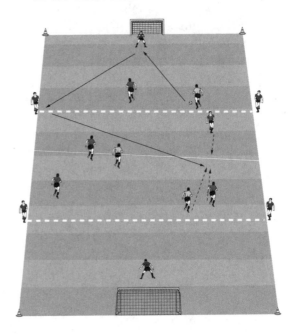

**ORGANIZATION:**
- Playing area measuring 30x40 yards with 2 big goals.
- There are three teams: one of six, one of five and one of three.
- The team of 6 consists of four outfield players and two goalkeepers.
- Each team wears its own colored vests.

**INSTRUCTIONS:**
- 9v5 positional game.
- The positional game is played by the team of three together with the team of six.
- The nine players play to retain possession.
- The team of five must try to win the ball and score in one of the two goals.
- The two goals are defended by the goalkeepers.
- After losing possession, the four lay-off players must not help the defenders.

# SMALL SIDED GAMES (9v9) **179**

**OBJECTIVE:**    Improving tactical play.

**ORGANIZATION:**
- Two teams of 9 players including goalkeepers.
- One fixed goal, and a portable goal on the edge of the other penalty area.
- The team that is coached plays 1:2:3:3; the other team plays 1:4:3:1 and always starts with the build-up.

- Organize the defense.
- Where and when to break up the build-up play? Have players 3 and 4 pressure the lay-off player 9 from the side.
- The role of the player who wins the ball. Always look forward, decide whether to pass forward or square, assess whether the opposing players are organized or not.
- The role of lay-off players 9 and 10. Lay-off player 9 as far forward as possible, with lay-off player 10 deeper; pass to players 7 and 11, who make forward runs.
- The role of players 7 and 11 when the ball is played forward, and the role of the players 6 and 8.

**OBJECTIVE:** Improving tactical play.

**ORGANIZATION:**
- Two teams of 11 players including goalkeepers.
- Play in blocks of 10-15 minutes.
- The dark team plays 1:3:2:3 and the light team 1:3:4:3.

**INSTRUCTIONS:**
Light team
- The players fall back behind the center line.
- The two strikers move square towards the flank where the ball is but do not immediately try to exert pressure on the ball.
- When the right back (2) runs forward with the ball, the striker (9) immediately pressures him.
- The central midfielder (7) comes to the flank where the ball is.
- The second striker (11) moves to cover the number (8) of the dark team.